VOL 2: YOUR DUALITY WITHIN

A Study of Your Two Distinct & Opposing Inner Voices

ANDERSON SILVER

ISBN-13: 978-1-9995273-4-1

Cover design by Renee Barratt, www.TheCoverCounts.com

Have a question for the author? Join the discussion on Twitter @YourManual & on Reddit u/yourusersmanual.

Access all of Anderson Silver's content (Articles and Podcasts) on patreon.com/AndersonSilver.

CONTENTS

PREFACE

"It is a shame for the soul to be first to give way in this life, before your body gives way."

- Marcus Aurelius

The following collection of thoughts are a continuation of the search for a tranquil and happy life from my previous work *Your User's Manual*. I would therefore recommend reading the previous book, which I consider to be Volume 1 of a three-book series. If you have not yet read *Your User's Manual*, however, you will still get the full insight intended for the reader from the following pages, as the tenets are stand-alone. It is my hope that *Your Duality Within* will leave you with an understanding of, appreciation for and motivation to reflect on your two distinct inner voices. This should, in turn, give you more answers and clarity in the pursuit of your own journey for a fulfilling and tranquil life.

Over the following pages, I will set out to answer some pressing questions you may have. Among them is "What are the two voices within, and why do they exist?" Spirit, logos, random electrical signals, a being of itself, whether it ascends into an afterlife or disappears into thin air, etc., the questions surrounding our spirit, soul or consciousness are diverse and controversial. It is *not* the purpose of this book to surmise or make suppositions as to which religious or philosophical theory is correct regarding where our spirit and consciousness came from or is going to. Rather, the goal is to point out the similarities between different belief systems and philosophies and to identify some common points and facts that we can all agree on regarding our consciousness. In other words, we will explore the point of overlap that is in the middle of the Venn diagram of humanity's various theories regarding consciousness.

Before proceeding any further, I would like to clarify some nomenclature. As is often the case with broad and conceptual discussions, nomenclature and semantics can become a senseless and needless point of disagreement. But as long as definitions are made clear in the onset, confusion on words and their meaning can be avoided, so as to remain focused on the ideas that are being presented and discussed. With that in mind, I would like to list below some terms and definitions I use throughout the series:

> **"Autopilot"** - The instinctive operating system of the animal body. This mind runs nonstop and is often in control, while our rational mind comes into play less often and only when it is triggered.

> **"Body's mind"** - The instinctive mind that is part of the vessel that is our bodies. It comes with built-in survival instincts. This term is interchangeable with **"Animal mind,"** the **"Vessel's mind,"** or the **"Primitive mind."**

> **"Consciousness"** - We do not yet have a definitive answer for what consciousness is. However, here I use

it as a term to describe the non-physical personality we have within us. This term is interchangeable with **"Spirit"** (It does not refer to a spirit in any theistic fashion), the **"Something more"** within, or the **"Soul."**

"Here and Now" - Your present moment in your present location. Your life can be summarized in a series of consecutive "Here and Nows."

"Rational mind" - The higher faculty within us all, a unique gift to human beings. This is the part of the brain that is currently engaged as you read this book, that can think conceptually and is forward-thinking and calculating. This term is interchangeable with **"Intelligent mind,"** the **"Ordinary mind"** (as in emotionless), or (later in the book) the **"Real You."**

Socrates' dictum "Know thyself" is a guiding principle to the study that follows. Again, my intention here is not to make a case as to what this "something more" is, where it comes from, or where it is going. It is merely to acknowledge that there *is* "something more" that this second personality within is what creates our duality, and to explore through science, philosophy and spirituality why this duality exists in the first place. We will further explore how to manage this duality within by looking at an overview of its study over thousands of years of human existence.

There are no promises here to make your life problem-free. Rather, this three-volume series urges you to examine the nature of your problems, what they are and where they come from. This is not armchair philosophy. It cannot be applied once with expected returns for perpetuity. Quick fixes are a pipe dream and good solutions (like anything good and worthwhile in life) take time and effort to achieve. Your goal is about getting down to basics and acting on them consciously in your lifelong journey of working towards a tranquil life.

If you are reading this book, then like many you asked yourself burning questions such as: "What is my purpose in life?" or "Who am I?" or "How can I live a good life?" To answer any one of these existential questions, one would have to touch upon, in part, all three of them. That being said, generally speaking, the main focus in *Your User's Manual* was to explore the first question. The next two are questions I shall explore in the following two volumes of the series. Here, in *Vol 2: Your Duality Within* I will explore the second question "Who am I."

> "Death lies heavy upon one who dies unknown to himself."
>
> - Lucius Annaeus Seneca

1 THAT BIZARRE FEELING

"Throw out your conceited opinions, for it is impossible
for a person to begin to learn what he thinks he already
knows."

-    Epictetus

By committing to reading this book, you have decided to take
another step down the path that is your journey towards the goal
of self-improvement and attaining a tranquil life. You might have
already read my previous work, *Your User's Manual*. If so, you will
recall that to move forward, often one must be willing to admit
how little they actually know about a particular subject matter.
Despite whatever preconceptions one might have about a given
topic, one must be able to accept their own ignorance of it before
they can be open to truly learning about it. As awesome as we
are on so many levels, it is no secret that as human beings, we
are prone to overestimate our understanding of the world and
(worse) our control over it. Our confidence in what we think we

know and our inability to acknowledge the true extent of our ignorance is often a barrier for furthering our understanding of it all.

> "Education is universal. We must teach people, especially our youth, the source of happiness and satisfaction. We must teach them that the ultimate source of happiness is within themselves. Not machine. Not technology. Not money. Not power."
>
> - Dalai Lama

To continue your betterment, you must endeavor to learn something new, different and value added by seeking out new teachers, philosophers, artists, books, etc. This is a tangible way in which one can take a step down the path of enlightenment. Not surprisingly, education is at the center of it all. We are not born with all the knowledge in the world. Rather, we obtain and absorb information over time. This is what is referred to as education.

We must be able to admit that we can be instinctively resistant to new ideas if we think we already know everything there is to know about a subject matter. As you delve into the subject of the duality within, many of your current precepts of *what is* will change, or at the very least, be challenged. If you keep a closed mind to it all, the time you spend reading and reflecting here will be for nothing, so you may as well put the book down and walk away right now. But if you chose to read the following pages with the intent of potentially expanding your understanding of the world and your reality, all I ask of you is to keep an open mind. Absorb the information presented here. Truly take it in and assimilate it, then at the end of the book make your own assessments and judgments and develop your opinions based on all the knowledge available to you.

> "If you would improve, submit to be considered without sense and foolish with respect to externals. Wish to be considered to know nothing; and if you shall seem to some to be a person of importance, distrust yourself."
>
> -   Epictetus

Let's put this to practice shall we: You are you...who else would you be? You have a job, or go to school...you have an identity in the society you live in and participate in it as a parent, child, partner, student, worker, coach, artist, etc. Those eyes you see staring back at you in the mirror and those hands you see holding your book are part of this unique individual and identity that you have come to recognize as "ME." Well, what if I told you that you are not who you think you are? What if I told you that you, quite literally, have a dual personality within? A duality that you are presently or formally unaware of? What if I told you that no matter how many times you have looked down at your body or have looked into a mirror in your lifetime, you have never actually seen your *real* self? How would that make you feel? Like I said, just keep an open mind and make your own judgments at the end of the book. I would wager that what you read over the next few chapters may leave you (pleasantly) surprised.

You and I have never met, yet I know something about you. You have (on more than one occasion) been in a situation where you did or said something and immediately regretted it afterwards. Perhaps after the fact, you cringed at how you could have made such a decision. Here is another scenario I'm sure you were in: You know it is wrong to get emotional over a certain situation, and when things around you are in equanimity you are able to keep your emotions in check. But when you are provoked or triggered, you forget about all this rational thought and turn into a beast you do not like. Sometimes, it may even feel like you are watching a train wreck of a disaster happen in slow motion, as an independent third party observer, a spectator watching yourself say or do things that you are not entirely happy about...yet you watch it happen to your own chagrin. Any of this sound familiar?

How did I know this about you? Simple: All human beings suffer from this same curse, and have spoken, sung and written about it since our earliest days. The irreconcilable nature of our duality within has been, and always will be, at the core of the human condition. For millennia, human beings have suffered from the split personality within that thinks one thing and feels another, that wants one thing and does another; that KNOWS one thing yet ACTS another.

So how on earth can you, a smart, calculating and intelligent Homo Sapiens, act in such a way that is so contrary to everything you know and believe in, while helplessly watching it happen like another person from behind a viewing pane? The answer is simple but unnerving: You feel this way because in fact you ARE watching it happen as another person from behind a viewing pane. The duality within is very real and is at the core of these behaviours. Over the following pages, I will outline many other ways in which this duality manifests itself, and how to *manage* it and use it to your advantage in working towards a tranquil life.

> "We have no control over our feelings. Emotions are spontaneous things that arise."
>
> - Archbishop Desmond Tutu

I specifically chose to use the word *manage* and not *control*. Much like becoming a Philosopher King[1], which yields tranquility in its pursuit and not in its (unattainable) destination, your inner duality can never be fully controlled, but tranquility can be attained in the pursuit of managing it. In philosophy, there are no one-time fixes that are applied mechanically. Much like all else that is good and worthwhile having in life, this lifelong journey takes time, effort, repetition and a systematic application of doctrines to attain worthy results.

> "Often people ask me for the quickest and best solution to a problem. This is impossible. You can have the quickest or you can have the best solution, but not both."
>
> - Dalai Lama

---

[1] *This is a reference to the pursuit of the life of a Philosopher King in chapter 1 from* Your User's Manual. *It is not the destination of attaining some sort of sagehood that brings one tranquility, but rather the journey in the pursuit of it.*

As a rational intelligent human being, you almost always know what the right thing to do is. You know you should not get upset over certain things, that you should not take things personally, that you should eat fresh whole foods instead of ordering pizza for takeout, that you should not sit on the couch and waste away in front of a TV screen, etc. You know the right thing to do, but the tough part is following through on what you know to be 100% right. So, what's stopping you?

> "Instead of being a good person today, you choose instead to become one tomorrow."
>
> -   Marcus Aurelius

The answer is in the excuses you give yourself. Do you tell yourself that you will *not* eat healthy? Or that you will *not* make good use of your time and instead waste it in front of a screen? No. You (or rather a part of you) know these to be wrong. Instead, you tell yourself "tomorrow...today I deserve this or need this...but tomorrow or soon I'll get on track." This is directly a result of your duality within: A voice within knows one thing, yet the body does another.

> "What then? Is it possible to escape error altogether? No, it is impossible: but it is possible to set one's mind continuously on avoiding error. For it is well worth while to persist in this endeavour, if in the end we escape a few errors, and no more. As it is, you say, 'I will fix my attention tomorrow': which means, let me tell you, 'Today I will be shameless, inopportune, abject: others shall have power to vex me: to-day I will harbour anger

and envy.' Look what evils you allow yourself. Nay, if it is well to fix my attention tomorrow, how much better to do so today! If it is profitable to-morrow, much more so is it today: that you may be able to do the same tomorrow, and not put off again to the day after."

- Epictetus

The next few chapters will discuss and answer some questions regarding your duality within. What is this duality within really? Where did it come from? Why does it exist? Does it have a purpose? If so, what is it? And is it possible to use this duality to your advantage in your ultimate goal of leading a tranquil life?

"So much suffering could be banished with the wave of a rational mind."

- Dalai Lama

2 A BRIEF HISTORY IN THE STUDY OF THE INNER DUALITY

Surprise! You have two voices within you. No, you are not losing your mind, or hearing voices. You really do have two conflicting and opposing minds working inside your brain. Believe it or not, the lack of cooperation between these two voices explains many of your mental afflictions. The following chapters will get into further details, but for now let us simply take a minute to remove the veil of dissolution on your world and acclimatize you to the existence of the two voices, who they are, how they came to be and what they are saying.

"You are a little soul carrying around a corpse."

\- Epictetus

The duality within is not some arcane or esoteric idea that just happened to come about. I am not a sage or a philosopher guru that just recently discovered this divide within through clairvoyance and meditation. No, the duality within has been a theme of stories, fables, songs, poems, philosophies, religion and all other domains of conceptual thought throughout human history. This introspective reflection on the duality within has existed almost as long as consciousness has existed among our species. In fact, you must have already seen it or been exposed to the idea of the duality within as this topic has also permeated common folklore. Let's look at a few such cases.

Something you are probably familiar with is the story of a protagonist that must make a difficult choice. He stands there contemplating his options…then *poof!* Out of nowhere appears a little figure on one shoulder cloaked in a red cape with reddish skin, horns and a barbed tail. Holding a pitchfork with a sinister smile, it whispers into the ear of our protagonist to do the selfish thing or take the easy way out. As the logic behind the argument of the little devil sinks in and the protagonist is convinced that it's okay to be selfish or greedy just this once…*poof!* Out of thin air appears an angel on the other shoulder. Equipped with a halo, maybe some wings and a harp, and wearing a white gown, the angel gives advice and arguments opposing those selfish ones of the little devil. The little angel urges our protagonist to do the right thing. This iconography of a traditional angel vs devil on either shoulder, arguing different sides of the decision is a Christian depiction of our duality within. There is one voice that wants to do what seems easy and fun even though it may be mischievous or bad. Then there is the other voice of reason, that knows it to be wrong and wants to do the right thing even though it may be harder or less profitable. *"You have had a rough*

9

day! Order your favourite pizza and relax on in front of the TV. After the day you've had, you deserve it!" "No don't eat takeout pizza in front of the TV...eat something healthy and go for a walk...your heart will thank you later!"

"There is something of a civil war going on within all our lives."

- Dr. Martin Luther King Jr

The philosophers of ancient Greece and Rome made a clear distinction between the faculty of reason (a gift from the gods that is our capacity for rational intelligent thought) and the animal vessel in which this consciousness and faculty of reason resides. Your rational intelligent mind (also referred to as the soul or spirit by the ancient philosophers) exists in this vessel (or the body) that has its own "wants" and impulses[2]. Most of the time, what the animal body's senses want is opposed to that which the rational mind knows to be right. This, again, is your duality within at work. *"But order the pizza anyway. It's just one day...it tastes delicious, you're tired and deserve to sit and relax in front of the TV*

---

[2] *This is a topic that was discussed in detail in chapter 9 of* Your User's Manual *titled "Bad Coding". The general idea is that emotions and knee-jerk reactions based on emotions are prebuilt "If," "Then," "Therefore" statements that are part of your core operating system. Some of it can never be changed as it is coded deeply in your DNA as evolutionary remnants of competitive advantages of our species and your ancestors. But there are some that are a product of your environment, education and upbringing. These can be changed overtime using simple exercises.*

after a long days' work!" "No, you would only regret it after you pig out and would feel bad and bloated in the morning. If you eat well and go for a walk you will feel so much better afterwards and you know it!"

> "In contemplating yourself, never include the vessel that surrounds you and these organs that are attached to it. For they are like an axe, differing only in this that they grow from the body. For indeed, without the cause that moves and checks them, there is no more use in these parts than in the weaver's shuttle, the writer's pen and the driver's whip."
>
> \- Marcus Aurelius

Sigmund Freud's body of work was revolutionary and is still a core doctrine in contemporary modern psychology. One of the central precepts in his body of work was his psychoanalytic theory of personality, which states that one's personality is composed of three parts: the id; the ego; and the super-ego. It generally states that the id is present from birth and includes instinctive and primitive behaviours. The ego, conversely, is the component of rationality dealing with the real world, based on a set of established moral standards. These higher moral standards are the super-ego. The id is the devil that wants to pursue a meaningless yet pleasurable and sensual encounter with an attractive person, and the ego under the guidance of the superego is the angel that reminds us that a momentary sexual escapade is worthless compared to the rewarding, spiritual and lifelong connection one has with their partner.

"It is a predisposition of human nature to consider an unpleasant idea untrue, and then it is easy to find arguments against it."

- Sigmund Freud

Another example from modern day psychology is Daniel Kahneman's studies of the duality within and its effects on our decision-making capabilities. His work has led to the creation of many new disciplines including decision sciences and even marketing[3] techniques. To more clearly present his research results and thesis, Kahneman fabricates two fictional characters named *System 1* and *System 2*. System 1 consists of an automated, almost unconscious, fast, impulsive, emotional and error-prone mind. System 2 is an effortful, slow, controlled and calculating mind that is reliable and can make complex decisions. In our context, System 1 is the body's mind that chases sensory wants, and System 2 is the rational mind that knows better.

"Pleasure deprives a man of the use of his faculties quite as much as pain."

- Socrates

---

[3] *Marketing is essentially an advanced form of psychological warfare. The assailants are the industry that spends more than a trillion dollars annually to entice the consumer to "want" their product. The corporate advertising industry, as we know it today, is the brainchild of Edward Bernays, who used his uncle Sigmund Freud's ideas to help implant ideas of "wanting" something in the viewers of his advertisements.*

Immanuel Kant spent his lifetime studying and dissecting the human nature in his thought experiments. Kant concludes that as human beings we find ourselves constantly in this state of being pushed and pulled around between two things – a faculty of reason and an animalistic desire. Sometimes we give in to those desires and sometimes we are able to use our capacity for reason to overcome them (overcome is the apt word here) and do the morally right and virtuous thing. This internal battle is part of our human nature and it is an inescapable aspect of being human.

> "Vice may be had in abundance without trouble; the way is smooth and her dwelling-place is near. But before virtue the gods have set toil."
>
> > > \- Glaucon (son of Ariston) in Plato's
> > > Republic

But Kant was far from being the only modern age philosopher to explore this duality. From Francis Bacon (1561-1626) to Albert Camus (1913-1960) and a multitude in between, many new age philosophers have also explored the duality within from their respective points of view. René Descartes presented his ideas on this duality in his famous work of the 'Mind-Body problem'. Georg Wilhelm Friedrich Hegel went so far in his studies between the duality of the faculty of reason and the animal mind, that he even developed an entirely new methodology for said studies (which is still used today) called *Hegel's Dialectic*. Arthur Schopenhauer's impressive body of work *The World as Will and Idea* clearly identifies (through case studies) the two different representations of the world: the intuitive and the abstract. The former is primitive and present at birth (*A Priori*[4]), and the latter constitutes complex though. Schopenhauer states that the capacity to perceive these conceptual representations is a gift to human beings alone (in the entire animal kingdom) and is called *reason*.

Across time and disciplines, the duality within keeps coming up in different studies. Moreover, one can look in the distance not only in time, but in space (geography) as well. Ever heard of this thing called Yin and Yang? It is the principle of the dualism in everything (including you) of the good and the bad, the contradictory sides that are always opposing yet completing each other. The theme of the duality within is also present in other far Eastern bodies of work such as Confucianism and goes as far back as the *Tao Te Ching*, written 2500 years ago by Lao Tzu, completely exclusive of the influence of ancient European philosophers.

"Then we may fairly assume that they are two [personalities within], and that they differ from one another; the one with which a man reasons, we may call the rational principle of the soul, the other, with which he loves and hungers and thirsts and feels the fluttering of any other desire, may be termed the irrational or appetitive, the ally of sundry pleasures and satisfactions."

- Socrates

---

[4] *Knowledge that is independent of all particular experiences, as in instinctively present.*

The ancients, the moderns, Easterners, Westerners, philosophers, theists, scientists, and more all came to the same inevitable conclusion. The duality within is unequivocally at the center of the human condition. There are endless stories and metaphors from different time periods, different cultures, and different corners of the globe regarding the duality within. The general theme of the (repeating) story is that we are constantly being pulled apart by competing desires and that it is impossible for anyone to do the right thing all the time. You are human. You will make mistakes. You will instinctively want/think/do things that are contrary to your faculty of reason. All you can do is try and do better next time, to try and act on what your rational intelligent mind knows to be right, to listen to that little angel on your shoulder and try as much as you can to do the right thing. Virtue is not about perfection but about reducing errors.

"Excellence is not a gift, but a skill that takes practice. We do not act 'rightly' because we are 'excellent', in fact we achieve 'excellence' by acting rightly."

- Plato

3 BELIEFS & ONTOLOGY

The duality within is an integral part of many schools of thought including religions, philosophies and even economic systems. The goal of this book is not to advocate for one school over the other but to draw on the similarities of the wide range of doctrines from different periods of human existence, different parts of the globe, and different viewpoints (i.e. definitions) of what it means to live a good life. The ultimate goal here is to help you better understand yourself. As far as your duality is concerned, you are not any more different than the other 100 billion Homo Sapiens who existed on this planet. Just like every single other person, you have an *inner discourse*. The inner discourse is the conversation (or debate) between the two voices within you representing the two different minds. *"Eat the pizza you deserve it!" "No don't eat the pizza, your long-term health deserves better!"* You can also rest assured that most of your fellow human beings (past or present) have had the same questions as you regarding this duality. Ever since human beings began to think introspectively about themselves, they noticed those parts of their own nature which seemed to "be there" from birth, despite lacking a physical form. This extra "something more" is distinctly separate and different from one's primitive and animalistic basic needs. The "something more" within us has a craving beyond the requirement for sustenance (food and water), propagation of the species (mating and socializing) and other basic physical needs.

As a matter of fact, you have felt this "something more" before. When life is swell and you have no immediate or urgent physical needs (i.e. you are feeling good and content), you have this inherent feeling to be more responsible towards those around you. Whether it be your friends, family or a complete stranger, we are all overcome with this sense of wanting to do something for others when we are not preoccupied with our own basic needs. Your animal instincts (e.g. hunger = eat food) are focused internally, but this feeling of wanting to do something nice externally is your "something more" speaking. Beyond fulfilling your basic physical necessities, it can be difficult to find something truly worthy of doing or pursuing in satisfying your life's meaning, which can leave an emotional, spiritual or existential "hole." This "hole" within is the direct cause of a struggle with one's existential discontent. Initially, one often tries to fill this hole with sensory pleasures (food, drink, drugs, sex, gaming, etc.) to generate and harbor a sensation of "life." But this always falls short. This sensory "high" is never long-lasting and comes with other consequences. We have all been there. It's not fun, it's hollow and we hate ourselves for being so clueless on how to live a fulfilling life.

> "The existential vacuum manifests itself mainly in a state of boredom...Sometimes the frustrated will to meaning is vicariously compensated for by a will to power, including the most primitive form of the will to power, the will to money. In other cases, the place of frustrated will to meaning is taken by the will to pleasure."
>
> - Viktor Frankl

Belief systems (whether political, social, religious, philosophical, or other) can be a delicate topic to discuss, given how polarizing and divisive they can be. But whatever school of thought you subscribe to, we can all agree on certain things. These points of agreement are what we must focus on to avoid getting lost in senseless debates over semantics. Our society spends so much time focusing on differences and criticizing others for having differing opinions. But we are all human beings who are more than 99.9% identical (genetically speaking). We all actually agree on much more than the few things we disagree on. For example, even if you are devoted to a cause that is completely opposed to what I believe in, we can both agree that stubbing your toe on the coffee table in the middle of the night on your way to the washroom is unpleasant. Sure, agreeing on the fact that in some diabolical fashion our pinky toes have evolved to find furniture in the dark is unpleasant and unwanted does not solve our existential crisis. But it is a simple and light-hearted reminder that we are identical biological organisms fighting (for the most part) the same fight.

> "In our quest for happiness and the avoidance of suffering, we are all fundamentally the same, and therefore equal."
>
> - Dalai Lama

Over and above the unpleasantness of stubbing one's toe, we can also agree that at times we all feel this emptiness inside, no matter how much fun we have in life. We can agree that ice cream is delicious, putting your feet up at the end of an exhausting day feels great, and that a cold beverage on a hot day is heavenly. We can further agree on the fact that we are alive right here and right now, and that we will cease to exist in this realm/dimension (in our current form) when we draw our last breath (regardless of what, if anything, happens next). We can agree that helping others, even something as simple as holding a door, just feels good. And we can agree that we are all in search of a good and tranquil life.

> "...tranquility is nothing else than the good ordering of the mind."
>
> - Marcus Aurelius

Ideologies (which includes today's social segregation based on title, money, status, social class, race, sexual orientation, ethnic background, nationality, etc.) will have us believe that we are all dissimilar from each other. Yet we have so much in common, much more than our differences. As the master economist shares in *The Wealth of Nations* (Book I Chapter II):

> "The difference of natural talents in different men is, in reality, much less than we are aware of...The difference between the most dissimilar characters, between a philosopher and a common street porter, for example, seems to arise not so much from nature as from habit, custom, and education. When they came into the world, and for the first six or eight years of their existence, they were perhaps very much alike, and neither their parents nor playfellows could perceive any remarkable difference."
>
> - Adam Smith

One of the many things we all share is the existence of this "something more" within us. No rational person can disagree that you (the real you – the intelligent mind that is focused on these words you are reading right now) exists. It is also self-evident that this, nonphysical "person" within us is separate from the physical vessel in which the "something more" resides[5].

---

[5] *Refer to the mental exercise in chapter 10 in* Your User's Manual. *A quick recap: When you put on a pair of prescription glasses to alter your vision, are you still you? What if you have a pacemaker inserted to regulate your heartbeat by changing it from the irregular one? What if you lose an arm due to a tragic accident? What if you lose all four limbs...are you still you? The reality is that no matter what happens to your physical body, you are still you. Therefore the "something more" you have must necessarily be independent and exclusive of your physical body.*

This we can agree on, even if we disagree on *where* this "something more" came from or *what* it may be (e.g. placed there by a creator, or evolved through natural selection, or was a pre-existing condition of the universe).

Whether this "something more" is a spirit, or is electrical signals bouncing around in neurons, or is part of a larger consciousness...whether this "something more" ascends into an afterlife, just disappears, or joins the rest of the consciousness in the universe, these are all up for debate (between differing belief systems and ontologies). However, as far as finding the answers we need to live a good tranquil life *today* is concerned, only one point is worthy of being noted: This "something more" within us definitely exists regardless of where it came from or where it's going. We have a body. The body can be acted upon. And we have an extra voice (this "something more") which is independent of, yet attached to, the body.

The body is easy to see. In fact, you have probably identified yourself as this squishy bag of puss and organs you call your body up until now. But the body (and its mind which we will get to soon) is only one of two voices you have within you. The voice of the "something more" within is the second part of your duality. It is the less obvious part to identify. When you look down, or look into a mirror, you can see your body. Moreover, it is easy to plainly understand that (for example) the feeling of *"I am hungry"* means food goes in the stomach, and then the thought of *"I am hungry"* is gone.

The second voice of the "something more" is the more intricate part and is less evident to identify. This more elusive and invisible part is the mind that thinks *"I may be hungry, but those poor kids look even hungrier, and I would rather share my loaf of bread with them than curb my own hunger."* This voice is the one we must learn to recognize and listen to, as it is the one that usually knows the right thing to do but gets lost in the *inner dialogue* (or the *inner discourse*).

The body's sensory wants are constant and loud. But we have this unique gift that allows us to think beyond mere physical and short-sighted cravings (*"I am hungry, eat the pizza!"*) so as to be able to make rational choices (*"Have a balanced healthy meal instead, it is more beneficial in the long run"*). And to our knowledge (so far) no other living being has been given this unique gift. So, let us explore what this gift is, what it says, where it came from and what it means to you.

4 WHAT IS THE INNER DUALITY REALLY?

You may not realize it, but you are a "value judgment" making machine. You win a $50 Amazon gift card in a raffle: You judge this as being good! You witness someone stealing a bike: You judge this as being bad. You have used your value judgments to support and justify all the decisions you have ever made in your entire life. All human beings feel morally justified in their decision making (yes...even the most illicit ones) and these decisions are all justified and supported by value judgments. Moreover, you are making these moral judgments (for the most part) without even consciously being aware of them. *"I'll have the multigrain toast with nut butter, because it's heart healthy."* This is justifying a healthy breakfast choice and feeling good about it. *"I'm having the worst morning and need a pick me up...this chocolate almond croissant is just what the doctor ordered."* This is justifying an unhealthy breakfast choice and feeling good/justified about it.

No matter the choice ("good" or "bad") you most definitely have a justification internally for them, before you take an action.

> "What decides whether a sum of money is good? The money is not going to tell you; it must be the faculty that makes use of such impressions – reason."
>
> - Epictetus

But if you are making value judgments from the moment you wake up until the moment you fall asleep, how come you are not aware of this constant evaluation and judgment of things? The answer is simple logistics. Actively engaging our higher capacity for reason to make conscious moral evaluations and decisions on each and every action we take would be exhausting to say the least. It would also grind our day to a halt, as we would be spending all our time contemplating moral dilemmas to make moral decisions. But fear not! Our body has a coping mechanism in the form of an "autopilot" that makes most of our decisions and moral justifications in split second evaluations and assessments.

So how does this "autopilot" work exactly? It uses an algorithm that is very straight forward: If a value judgment was made on something in the past with acceptable results, then repeat the same value judgment under similar parameters. As an example, at some early point in your life, you had a moral reflection on whether it is a good idea for you to put your opposite foot forward, as you lean forward, to continue the motion of walking as opposed to falling down. As comical as this contemplation may be (and the image of a you slowly falling flat on your face whilst trying to make a decision on whether it is a "good" or "bad" idea to put your foot forward or not) this is something your brain actively thought of when you were learning to walk as a toddler. And look at you today! You can walk without having to think about it you champ! Everything you do that is part of your "routine" today (including repeating the motion of walking when you want to move forward) is done without questioning the moral necessity or righteousness of the action. You just do it because you've always done it thus (e.g. If you are a coffee drinker, do you think about grabbing that first cup of coffee "to get going" in the morning?). But at one point, each action in your routine was a new action and thus was subjected to the consideration of whether it would be "good" or "bad" to do it.

"We first make our habits, and then habits make us."

- John Dryden

Today, you only take the time to make serious moral contemplations when there is a big decision on the line: "Should I change my career? Get divorced? Move to another country?" etc. But for some reason you don't perform this moral contemplation for the little things: "Should I grab that mug that is falling? Should I walk faster since it began to rain? Should I drink this water since I'm thirsty?" These contemplations all belong in the domain of your "autopilot." There is nothing wrong with relying on the "autopilot" and its ongoing decisions, as our lives would be paralyzed otherwise in trying to contemplate decisions all day. However, this does raise a series of significant questions: How many of these "autopilot" decisions are being made without you being aware of it? Are these automatic decisions the right ones? Who is this "autopilot"? Why do some people seem to rely more on this "autopilot" (just go with the flow) and others feel the need to have an internal philosophical debate over everything prior to making a decision (try and control everything)? Where do you fall on this bell-curve? And most importantly, how do you feel now that you begin to realize that a great majority of your life has been based on decisions made by an "autopilot"…while you were blissfully unaware?

This "autopilot," which is responsible for the great majority of your life's decisions, is part of your body's animal mind. The active decisions you make that take longer, where you contemplate different variables, outcomes and mull over them (for several days sometimes) is your rational mind at work. So, the next natural question is how many decisions has your animal mind taken, that your rational mind would now disagree with in retrospect? I'm sure you can think of more than a few occasions where you did something and after the fact (in hindsight) seriously questioned your own decision-making paradigm.

The control of your attention is shared by your two minds within. At any given moment only one of the two minds can be in the driver's seat of your ruling faculty. Imagine you're at a party and are having a conversation with someone. All of a sudden you hear a loud offensive comment on the other side of the room. Out of proper decorum, you may be able to resist turning toward the source of the loud comment when it is blurted out. However, even if your head doesn't turn and you do your best to try and stay engaged in the conversation you are having, your attention will initially be directed towards the commotion, at least for a little while. The real you (or the rational mind that is engaged in the conversation) cannot help this shift in focus. This is not due to a shortcoming or failure of your rational intelligent mind. The change in focus has to do with a built-in response mechanism that is part of your body. It can override your rational mind in an instant and very effectively shut it out to engage its own primitive mind. It becomes the "driver" of your ruling faculty without you ever realizing it.

Both minds (or voices) live inside the same physical brain and body. Our bodies are a part of nature, so both minds are a part of nature as well. One thing that is glaringly evident in nature is that everything seeks the path of least resistance. Your body's mind and your rational mind are no exception to this. For example, if you are going through a very bad time, the body's animal mind wants to be sad, self-loathing and feel pity for itself. It just wants to stay home and hide under a blanket to avoid the sadness that is outside. It wants to act the way it feels without any consideration for the future, as this is its path of least resistance. Your rational mind, however, wants to fight through this emotional sensation. Unlike the short-sighted primitive mind, it recognizes the feelings of sadness, but it also recognizes the need to go out and provide for itself as it will need to eat and have bills to pay. It is not willing to jeopardize its future and cause harm for itself in the long run, due to an overreaction today. This is the rational mind's path of least resistance.

The two paths of least resistance differ mainly in the timescale of the frame of reference that they use. The animal brain thinks only in the immediate sensory feelings and wants (it is the one who wants to have the sexual relations with the attractive mate that walks by). Whereas the rational mind thinks in the longer term as it is aware of its continued existence beyond the immediate (it is the one that considers the fulfilling, rewarding and beneficial relationship with its partner, as opposed to jumping in bed with the attractive mate for a momentary enjoyment of pleasure). As much as these two voices are opposed, they are both very much alive and active in your mind and affect your decision-making capabilities in their own way. And this "debate" between the two minds is your inner discourse.

> "It's not what you say out of your mouth that determines your life, it's what you whisper to yourself that has the most power."
>
> -   Robert Kiyosaki

You can visualize the discourse between the two minds: Both of them sitting at a table, opposing one another...one gesticulating and spewing with emotions...the other cool, calm and collected, asking its disheveled counterpart reasonable, rational and intelligent questions. Which one do you want to be? Both are inside you, but you ultimately have the choice of deciding who commands your ruling faculty.

5 WHY YOU HAVE A DUALITY PART I –
YOUR BODY'S (ANIMAL) MIND

How or where life came from is a great mystery to which we do not yet have a definitive answer. But thanks to fossil evidence, we can estimate that life (in the form of bacteria and archaea[6]) appeared on earth about 3.8 billion years ago. Then 1.8 billion years ago eukaryotes came into existence, which were the first cells with rudimentary internal organs. Some 1.3 billion years ago eukaryotes divide into the three familiar groups of plants,

---

[6] *In the study of life (biology) we use a domain system introduced by Carl Woese in 1977 that divides life into three categories of cellular composition. The three domains (main branches of the tree of life) are: bacteria (basic single-celled organisms with no cell nucleus); archaea (also single-celled organisms with no cell nucleus but with a different cellular wall, genetic make-up, and protein structures); and eukaryotes (organisms with cells containing a nucleus).*

animals and fungi. About 525 million years ago, the first animals with a backbone (vertebrae) evolves. Fast forward to about 2.5 million years ago when the genus *Homo* evolves from a common ancestor with chimpanzees or bonobo monkeys, then a little over 150,000 years ago the first Homo Sapiens evolved in the plains of South-East Africa...and then you were born.

Some of these general "guesses" in evolution are backed up by fossils and scientific evidence, though there are many extrapolations and "best-guesses" in this timeline. The biggest mystery of course is where and how it all began and there are many theories ranging from panspermia to life spontaneously evolving from the primordial soup[7]. But there is one thing that all of us can agree on: Life somehow appeared on earth and is still here today. We also can see from biological evidence that life is very adaptable and has found a way to adjust to its changing environment. This is why life can be found in all reaches of the planet and has survived countless catastrophes throughout history, ranging from ice ages, to meteor strikes and killer volcanoes.

These adaptations and changes have led to the different species that we observe today. Each different species lives in a different environment or is sustained by a different source of nutrition. Therefore, each species has varying tools and skills to be able to survive its respective challenges in its habitat. We humans are no exception to this, so we would not be alive without these

---

[7] *This is in reference to the heterotrophic theory of the origin of life.*

adaptive (evolutionary) changes and built-in skills that come from these adaptations. What are these skills you ask? Are you breathing right now? I sure hope so! Assuming you are, here's another question: Do you have to think about breathing? Can you imagine living your life constantly having to think *"Okay time to breathe in now…Okay time to breath out now."* Think about all the intricate systems within you that works like a machine to turn oxygen into molecules you need to stay alive. Imagine having to consciously direct your thoughts to breath in and out repetitively *and* actively move all the necessary parts of the machine that is your respiratory system in the exact order of the choreography that turns air outside your body into crucial molecules inside your body. Just thinking about it is exhausting! If we did not have the built-in automated skills to do all this naturally (as in without having to actively think about it), best case scenario we would be drained from keeping up with our breathing routine, and worst-case scenario we would die from suffocation.

So let us first and foremost acknowledge that thanks to our ancestors' adaptations to their respective environments, we do MANY MANY things that are necessary for our survival without having to actively think about them (way to go first fish that grew autonomous lungs that work on land!). But modern times have brought comfort, security and redundancies. As a result, some old evolutionary traits are no longer necessary for survival. For example, let's talk about eyesight. Our ancestors would have needed 20/20 vision to have the best chance of survival. A lion in the Savanna is hard to dodge if you think there's a cute fuzzy bush in the distance instead of recognizing that a predator is running at you. Today, more than half the population is lacking 20/20 vision, but people do not die from it. Most vision deficiencies are easily fixed with glasses, lenses or surgery. A fully functioning heart would have been another must have for our ancestors. In the past, an offbeat (no pun intended) sinoatrial node would have led to heart failure and immediate death. Today, we just throw a pacemaker in there to regulate the heartbeat. What used to be a fatal flaw and a guaranteed death sentence is now an easy fix with a fairly common surgery. There are hundreds of other examples of physical necessities our ancestors needed for survival that are no longer necessary for us to survive today.

This phenomenon is not limited only to physical aspects. Ever saw something fly towards you (like a ball) from your peripheral vision and flinched? We all have. Have you ever stopped to consider that we all flinch in the same way (raise, bend and tighten your arms around you), yet we have not been taught this? It is because of instinct. Our instinct is to cover and shield our vital organs in the face of a perceived threat, so we turn our arms and forearms into shields and cover our core as much as possible. Closing your eyelids...same thing. If something is flying towards your precious eyes, you will try and protect them by turning your head away and closing your eyelids tight. We ALL do this...not because of a mandatory "How to Flinch" bootcamp we attended as infants, but because these are part of the genetic (psychological) coding we have in us from millions of years of evolution and adaptation to our environment...just like breathing without thinking.

As important as these natural psychological instincts are, many of them have become obsolete in today's modern world (much like the case on the physical side of things). For example, today we immediately associate pessimism as a negative personality trait. However, in our long genetic history, pessimism was an important trait to have. If you instinctively thought more negatively, you survived. One example where being pessimistic would have helped you survive is if you were naturally scared due to your negative disposition of your environment, instead of being curious (i.e. being jumpy) you were the first to run when something was heard rumbling in the bush. On the occasion where that rumbling was a lion, you would have been putting other "bodies" between you and the predator, so you survived longer to pass on your genes.

Pessimism (as much as you hate it today) was a key survival instinct that our ancestors developed as part of an on-going defense mechanism going back over half a billion years[8] to survive. But the survival benefits of pessimism does not stop with predators. How about food? If you were more doubtful about food reserves, you hoarded more food and would survive that freak winter that lasted longer. If you were less adventurous

---

[8] *Ediacaran biota is the oldest fossil evidence of an organism that first began to grow "countermeasures" against its environment, which includes its predators. Specifically, Ediacaran biota had a hard shell and exoskeleton, and the fossils date back about 550 million years ago. Some of the fossils of these earliest exoskeletons are punctured with circular holes about 0.4 mm across, which suggest they were penetrated with a predator's teeth.*

about trying that thing that may or may not be edible, you didn't get poisoned (the second mouse gets the cheese). The myriad of examples where pessimism was a beneficial survival mechanism for our ancestors goes on.

Fine...that horrible thing we call pessimism (which manifests itself in a series of emotions including fear and jumpiness) was useful for survival in the past. But think about the instinct of pessimism and anxiety you have today. How's that treating you? Probably not great. Do you think you still need it? We have global food supplies, redundant distribution systems, and inventories. Death from famine is at a historical all-time low (at least for human beings). There is still violence and local conflicts here and there, but the great majority of human beings today live in secured peaceful nations governed by laws with minimal risk of predatory assaults. Deaths at the hands of predators (including other human beings) is also at a historical all-time low. So, these primitive animal instincts for a pessimistic disposition we have are no longer useful, necessary or beneficial for survival. Most would agree that, today, pessimism and anxiety cause more problems than they save lives[9].

---

[9] *As per the Anxiety and Depression Association of America (ADAA), 1 in 5 adults suffer from Anxiety disorders, which is the most common mental illness in the United States. Similar numbers are reported by the various groups in the UK and France. Mental disorders from anxiety and depression are currently an epidemic that we face as a species.*

So, the primitive mind (the body's mind) has many obsolete instincts as part of its core operating system. How did this happen? Why do we have these instincts (still) if we no longer need them anymore? It all began 70,000 years ago with the Cognitive revolution. Although the Agricultural and Industrial (and its conjoined twin the Scientific) revolutions get all the attention, the impact of the Cognitive revolution is unmatched. It had tremendous implications on the existence of life (all life) on this planet. Specifically, for our species, the Cognitive revolution gave our ancestors the capacity for conceptual thought, which led to two major changes: 1) communication as a competitive advantage; and 2) out evolving natural selection.

As far as our Sapiens ancestors' physical capabilities were concerned, the Neanderthals were superior pretty much in every way. Although humans in general were on top of the food chain before Sapiens evolved, in inter-human species conflict Sapiens simply could not compete with the physical superiority of the Neanderthals. In fact, the first time the two species met in the Arabian Peninsula about 100,000 years ago, we were soundly beaten and retreated back to the plains of South East Africa[10]. But then the Cognitive revolution came to pass and Sapiens began their march North a second and definitive time. Not only did our ancestors successfully make it past the Arabian Peninsula

---

[10] *The first recorded encounter between Sapiens and Neanderthals was about 100,000 years ago when Sapiens migrated north to the Levant but failed to secure a foothold. It might have been due to aggressive natives, climate, parasites, etc., but Sapiens did not survive this first migration attempt and retreated back south.*

this time, but they kept on marching to every single corner of the planet. In the process, they killed off (willingly or unwillingly) all existing human species. Neanderthals were the last ones to go extinct about 30,000 years ago[11]. So essentially, in a mere 40,000 years, we went from being a physically inferior ho-hum sub-set of the human species roaming the south-east plains of Africa to being the apex predator (including other human species) in the entire planet. How did this overwhelming change in fortune happen?

When you think "conflict superiority," one naturally jumps to the conclusion that Sapiens must have had some technological advantage from the use of a tool, weapon or fire that allowed them to conquer the planet. However, all human species had tools, spears and fire. In fact, fire was domesticated by humans 800,000 years ago, well before Sapiens even evolved 150,000 to 200,000 years ago. Most anthropologists now agree that Sapiens' tools or weapons were not unique and sophisticated enough to give such a dominant edge to our ancestors. Instead, the key to our incredible success lies in our secret weapon: communication.

---

[11] *Two theories exist regarding how other human species went extinct. One is referred to as the interbreeding theory, which suggest the different species interbred with the Sapiens (as Sapiens spread throughout the world) and genetically assimilated into our ancestors' evolutionary line. The second more sinister replacement theory suggests that other species were killed off in conflicts with our Sapiens ancestors in a form of interspecies genocide.*

"Communication   leads   to   community,   that   is
understanding, intimacy and mutual valuing."

-    Rollo May

You use this powerful capacity all the time. In fact, you are using
it right now as you read these words and receive my organized
thoughts. Between television, radio, internet, social media,
books, conversations, etc., you give, receive and process
terabytes of data every day. This incredible capacity for
communication that we possess finds its roots in the Cognitive
revolution. Until that point, it is believed that the human species
communicated through grunts and very basic sign language only.
So, the Sapiens (just like their main competition for supremacy -
the Neanderthals) were limited to organizing smaller hunting or
fighting groups. The transfer of information was very limited
and therefore basic in nature. This basic level of communication
can be observed in other animals today including wolves that
howl to call other pack members, fireflies that blink to attract
mates, elephants that use their trunks to talk to other herds over
long distances, baboons who use touch to show affection, etc.

Following the Cognitive revolution, however, Sapiens gained the
capacity to have more complex communication through more
complex sounds, drawings, markings, signals, etc. This gave our
ancestors a tremendous competitive advantage in being able to
organize in larger groups and plan ahead. And so, even though
our ancestors may have been inferior in a one-on-one fight,
through communication, they organized the largest numbers at
arms and became the apex predator who drove most large game

and all other human species to extinction across the planet[12]. At this point in the book, we do not need to keep exploring the evolution of communication, however, it is important to outline that the capacity for complex communication was merely a by-product we gained from the capacity for conceptual thought (a key and significant product of the Cognitive revolution).

The newly gained capacity for conceptual thought is the driver behind everything that modern man has accomplished. We can dream, imagine and think beyond the "Here and Now." This capacity is unique to only us Sapiens out of all the living creatures in the plant and animal kingdom (as far as we know today). This capacity for conceptual thought has a tremendous effect on us and our evolutionary path (both up until now and going forward). We will explore this unique gift we have and its implications on our lives in the following chapter.

The second important change that came about during the Cognitive revolution was the process of evolution itself. For the first time in more than 3 billion years, adaptation to one's environment (or evolution) was no longer only through physical mutations. Evolution used to be a slow and painstaking process of natural selection of random physical mutations leading to

---

[12] *To be fair to our ancient Sapiens ancestors, we do not yet know if the other human species were hunted and killed in a form of interspecies genocide or if they simply died out slowly due to us being better at hunting and gathering resources from shared territories, driving them to famine. The most likely answer, as always, is probably a mix of both.*

competitive advantages. Following the Cognitive revolution, however, evolution accelerated and became a function of mental capacities and imagination (that is as it pertains only to our species).

Only 25,000 years after our ancestors left (for the second time) the plains of South East Africa, Sapiens made it across ocean waters from the Siam peninsula to the continent of Australia. Achieving the capacity to traverse this body of water did not take us hundreds of millions of years to physically evolve into a specimen that could traverse water. Homo Sapiens did not mutate back into an aquatic animal and evolve gills to swim there, neither did they evolve into aeronautical animals and grow wings to fly across the vast bodies of water. Physically speaking, for all intents and purposes the Sapiens that stepped foot on the continent of Australia were the same as the ones who walked north out of the planes of South-East Africa. So how did we do it? Simple: We built boats because we could imagine them and build them thanks to our capacities of conceptual thought.

A mere 150,000 years later, we have conquered all reaches of the planet's rocky surface, the seas, under the sea, the skies, and even space as we have a permanent space station and have sent human beings to the Moon. None of this was as a result of physically evolving to adapt to the environment through natural selection, but due to the capacities of our own imagination (and capacity for complex conceptual thought). Almost 4 billion years of life on this planet, and no other species has been able to live beyond an environment it had physically evolved to survive in...*ever*. This is incredible and beyond a doubt the most amazing achievement of our species.

Unfortunately, this also presents a bleak outlook for our species, as evolving *with* your environment means living in symbiosis with it as well. Every other form of life that thrived (and note the virus is not fully accepted as being a form of life[13]) has therefore always naturally and instinctively lived in harmony with its environment. We on the other hand, live to accomplish our dreams, and use whatever we can from our environment to fuel it with complete disregard for its short or long-term impact on ourselves or the environment we live in.

So far, we have been able to stay ahead of this destructive pattern. Our intelligence, ambition and creativity have found ways to reach further into the realm of the impossible and find different ways to compensate for the damage we do to ourselves (as a species) and our environment. Polluting the water? No problem, invent water filters. Running out of raw materials? No

---

[13] *According to the most commonly accepted definition, life is "an organismic state characterized by capacity for metabolism, growth, reaction to stimuli, and reproduction." Although viruses are complicated assemblies of molecules, proteins, nucleic acids, lipids, and carbohydrates, without entering other living cells viruses cannot multiply. Given their natural incapacity to reproduce, viruses are not generally considered to be living things.*

problem, learn to recycle. CO_2 emissions from burning fossil fuels causing severe air pollution and the greenhouse effect? No problem, invent and invest in alternative energy sources. To date, we remain ahead of the curve of self-destruction thanks to our ingenuity, complex conceptual thought and resourcefulness. For our species' sake, we can only hope this trend continues.

6 WHY YOU HAVE A DUALITY PART II – YOUR RATIONAL MIND: ENTER "CONSCIOUSNESS"

"A human being is part of the whole called by us 'Universe'; a part limited in time and space. He experiences himself, his thoughts and feelings as something separated from the rest - a kind of optical delusion of his consciousness."

- Albert Einstein

This body (and its mind) you have today is a beautiful and magical amalgamation of historical events and transformation leading to nothing short of a miracle of nature. However, we also recognize that: 1) the body's mind is outdated in many ways; and 2) we acknowledge that there is this "something more" beyond this physical body and its own instinctive mind. René Descartes put it simply and succinctly when he said that since we can clearly conceive of the mind existing without the physical body, and vice versa, they cannot possibly be one thing. In my previous work *Your User's Manual,* I present a mental exercise (the ship of Theseus)[14], which allows the reader to very simply recognize that their self-identified "ME" is completely independent of the body. What you see in the mirror and what you see when you look down at your hands and arms is not all of you. There is "something more" inside this vessel thinking, perceiving and existing independent of your body. This is commonly referred to as your consciousness[15].

There are a myriad of theories out there as to how our consciousness came to be. Most theories fall within three broad categories – causal, teleological or intentional. The causal theory's general claim is that consciousness arose from the elementary building blocks of the universe requiring nothing more than the laws of nature as science teaches us today. What this means is that consciousness is simply random electrical signals shooting around in the collection of neurons, which exist in the carbon-based organ called the brain. The causal theory

---

[14] *This is a reference to the mental exercise in chapter 10 of* Your User's Manual. *No matter what happens to your physical body (mechanical additions or loss of organic body parts), you are still you. This is because the body is separate from the mind.*

[15] *Recall that we do not yet have an agreed upon definition of consciousness or what it is. For the purposes of this book we are using the word "consciousness" as the definition of the higher faculties of thought, reason, rationality, etc. It can be used interchangeably (in this book) with spirit or soul or rational intelligent mind in reference to the "something more" within.*

essentially states that consciousness came into existence due to the pre-existing conditions as we see them, as a result of natural evolution, following the laws governing the behaviour of the elements (i.e. the laws of nature).

Teleological theories postulate that in addition to the laws governing the behaviour of the elements that we can observe, there are additional principles of self-organization (governance) of the development of consciousness that is not explained by those elemental laws. In other words, in the same way we can observe matter and know some of its properties (e.g. laws of gravity), consciousness is its own element and has also always existed in different forms. We just can't directly observe it (yet) so we don't know any of its properties. However, consciousness found its way onto this planet (just as organic life did) and found the right conditions to exist in our brains.

Last but not least, the proponents of the theory of the intentional nature of consciousness state that our consciousness comes from an intervention by a being not limited by the laws of nature (presumably a God), who put the fundamental elements together in the right way to create consciousness. In other words, consciousness is specifically made and created for us by an omnipotent being, as a gift, to have and employ during our temporal existence here on earth. This unique gifting of our consciousness is common ground for most proponents of the intentional nature of consciousness, although different religions will disagree on *why* that is, *which* God gave it and *what happens to it* after death.

"[On mankind "sharing" his religious beliefs] He has made a graveyard of the globe in trying his honest best to smooth his brother's path to happiness and heaven."

-   Mark Twain

Many arguments have been had, unnecessary wars have been fought, and countless lives were lost over the simple disagreements of where our consciousness comes from, where it is going, and why exactly it exists. But beyond the disagreements there are many points of agreement as well, and that's where you will find the answers you seek. What are the points of agreement? We have this "something more" over and above the physical. With this "something more," we gained the capacity to discover (through reason) the truth about a reality that extends vastly beyond initial experience and perception (i.e. we can imagine things, predict things, discover the laws of nature, etc.). From these simple points of agreement, we can draw three very important conclusions:

1. We *all* have this "something more," which we can refer to as our consciousness.

2. Our consciousness lives in this vessel that is our animal body.

3. The animal body and the consciousness have different building blocks, perspectives and needs (immediate and otherwise), and so they each want or crave something different.

Your consciousness and its own wants, desires and thoughts are an inescapable component of your reality, which is not yet describable by the physical sciences. We ourselves are formations of matter and complex instances of something both objectively physical from outside (body and its primitive mind) and subjectively felt from inside (consciousness and your rational mind).

Ultimately, we are (as at the date of this book being written) entirely dependent on our animal bodies. This vessel may get damaged, but it usually heals itself. If not, we may find workarounds to fix it (glasses, pacemakers, prosthetics, medicine, etc.). But what happens to the vessel does not change the way you think...or at least, it does not change it directly (more on this in a later chapter).

You – the real you – is your consciousness living inside this animal vessel's brain (the organ), which also has its own thoughts (the animal mind). And although your capacity for thought is far superior to the body's inherent capacities as far as complexity and intelligence is concerned, the body's mind's instincts control many of the automated responses that hijack the overall computing power of the whole organ of the brain that both the body's mind and your rational mind share.

"Two elements are combined in our creation, the body, which we have in common with the beasts; and reason and good judgment, which we share with the gods. Most of us tend toward the former connection, miserable and mortal though it is, whereas only a few favour this holy and blessed alliance."

- Epictetus

You have a body and it has its own mind. This mind is nothing like your own rational mind that is intelligent and reasonable. The animal obstructs you from living a tranquil life. At this point, the logical conclusion that shutting out the animal brain is the key to your salvation and the secret to a happy life seems reasonable. Oh, if only it were that simple. There is no shutting out, shutting off, or suppressing the animal brain. Recall that due to simple energy conservation, the animal mind is active more often than your rational mind. So, the quest is not shutting out the animal brain but learning how to trigger your rational mind when *you* want to.

The animal brain will always want to have relations with the attractive mate that walks by. You (your rational mind), on the other hand, can counter this instinct with logical reasons. Your rational mind will think of the love, respect and bond you have with your partner, and dismiss the temporary flashes of lust the animal mind throws into your inner discourse. Neither can you shut out your instincts, nor can you turn them off. Instead you must learn to live together, honestly and with mutual respect. It is a symbiotic relationship that can be very beneficial to both minds if treated correctly. But if unattended, like any other relationship, the two voices within will have conflicts, breakdowns and spill over into other areas of your life.

> "I understand there's a guy inside me who wants to lay in bed, smoke weed all day, and watch cartoons and old movies. My whole life is a series of stratagems to avoid, and outwit, that guy."
>
> - Anthony Bourdain

7 THE REAL YOU

"This that I am, whatever it be, is a little flesh and breath, and the ruling part."

- Marcus Aurelius

I have news for you: You have never seen your true/real self and will never have the opportunity to do so. If the real you is your consciousness/your faculty of reason/ your rational intelligent mind that lives within the fleshy bits of your vessel, then you have never actually seen yourself. All you have ever seen is your bio suit. Look down at your legs and answer me this: If you had an accident and tragically lost your legs tomorrow...would you cease to be you? Of course not. You would still be "you," albeit with reduced mobility, but you would remain "you" because the vessel in which you reside is independent from who you truly identify yourself to be.

"Upon what depends the identity of the person? Not upon the matter of the body; [the body] is different after a few years,...which proves that in spite of all changes time produces in him something in him remains quite untouched by it. But [the conscious mind] which, unaltered always, remains quite the same, and does not grow old along with the surface. It is really the kernel of our nature, which does not lie in time. It is assumed that the identity of the person rests upon that of consciousness."

- Arthur Schopenhauer

You live in this vessel that possesses certain capacities for sensory inputs in the form of sight, hearing, smell, taste and touch. These capacities for perception and sensory inputs are marvels of biological engineering. As advanced as we are in robotics today, we are still light years away from replicating all the mechanics, sensory inputs, and intuitive cerebral calculations and processing that is required to manage all this data. But as impressive as these sensory inputs are, they are grossly limited in the cosmic scale of things. Thanks to our capacity for conceptual thought, modern day sciences have surmised and proven (through the language of mathematics) that multiple dimensions (up to 11 so far) exist. They have also shown that despite our lack of capacity to sense them, many invisible fields (electrical, magnetic, gravitational, etc.) exist, that most of what is out there is not yet visible or detectable (dark matter, dark energy, etc.), and that spacetime is a fabric (not separate variables). Using conceptual thought and abstract thinking, science has discovered and proven many other bizarre facts that we can't easily wrap our heads around. This is because ever since the Cognitive Revolution, our animal bodies' physical capabilities of perception (among other things) have not been able to keep up with our minds' capacity for conceptual thought and imagination.

Our vessel's eyes, which are a miracle of nature, cannot perceive anything beyond two things: Physical fields and a very small cross section of the electromagnetic spectrum (which we call colors). Look at the book in your hands. We know that it is made of atoms, and we know that atoms are 99.99% empty space. Yet the book you hold is not 99.99% see through. This is because our eyes have a capacity to view physical fields created by matter. Some fish have the capacity to sense electric fields, some birds have the capacity to sense magnetic fields...humans have the capacity to sense physical fields. (You can see, touch and feel the physical field of the book that is supposedly 99.99% empty space, right?)

Here's another mental exercise to demonstrate the limitations of your vessel's capacities for perceiving its environment. We live in a three-dimensional world, but let us go down one dimension and move to a hypothetical two-dimensional world (that would be like living on the surface of a sheet of paper). Imagine you were a two-dimensional being, living in a two-dimensional surface where all you would be able to see is right in front of you. You can't look up or down (there is no "up" or "down") but can pivot around a point to see around you in a circle. There are also other two-dimensional beings on the same plane as you. So, if we were all squares living on this flat plane then all you would see is different lengths of lines as you looked at "someone else." Only by walking around someone and noting the lengths of lines and outside angles of corners could you determine the shape and size of something. Again, since there is no "up" or "down" in a two-dimensional world, there would be no bird's-eye view or any way in which to see the whole shape of other beings, other than the single line facing you.

Now imagine an alien being that is a three-dimensional pyramid (like the pyramids of Giza) comes through our flat two-dimensional world. If this three-dimensional (alien) object were to travel through our two-dimensional world from top to bottom, we would never see it approaching in our little world. This alien would simply appear out of thin air when its base (the first cross section to hit our surface) touches and enters our two-dimensional (plane) world.

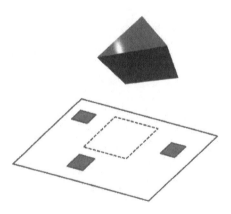

The pyramid descends from above (the "up" that the squares can't see). From the vantage point of the square citizens of this world, when the base touches the surface of the plane, the pyramid would manifest itself as a large square appearing out of thin air.

52

As the first cross section would hits this two-dimensional world, the local scientists would walk around, take measurements, and conclude that this alien being was a large square that appeared out of nowhere. They wouldn't know it descended from above, nor can they see the rest of the three-dimensional shape that is yet to go through the plane. But then the pyramid would keep moving downwards through the two-dimensional plane, and so the cross section (that is a square) would get smaller and smaller. The scientists would conclude the alien square is shrinking. Then the pyramid would keep travelling all the way through until the last cross section, a point, would appear on this surface, then disconnect from the bottom. The local two-dimensional scientists would have to conclude that this square alien appeared out of nowhere, then shrunk into a single point and disappeared or died. They wouldn't see, understand or know anything beyond that.

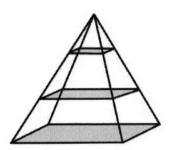

A pyramid travelling through a perfectly flat two-dimensional space from north to south (i.e. first the pyramids base would enter the plane, and the tip would be the last to touch it) would yield consecutive cross sections of squares, starting with the largest (the base) and ending with the smallest near the peak. The whole thing would end on a single point at the tip.

The visual of the three-dimensional pyramid travelling through a two-dimensional surface and the perspective of the square citizens of this two-dimensional world makes sense to you. You understand it, because you can visualize it since your animal body and its tools of perception operate in three dimensions. But can you imagine the confusion of the two-dimensional beings watching this from their reality? How would you go about explaining what happened to these two-dimensional beings that can't see and don't understand "up" or "down"?

Now let's change our exercise from one dimension down (two dimensions) to one dimension up (four dimensions) from our own reality. Our scientists, with their capacity for abstract thought, are able to conceptualize some shapes in four dimensions. We even have names for them. One such shape is called the Tesseract. For the purpose of introducing the Tesseract, let us go through the dimension from the starting point of zero. A point in space is called a dot and has no dimensions. Two dots that are connected to form a one-dimensional object is called a "line." Four equal lines joined at 90-degree angles is a two-dimensional object called a "square." Six squares that form a three-dimensional object is called a "cube" (so far you're with me right?). And eight cubes that form a four-dimensional object is called a Tesseract. We know how the Tesseract (also called a Hypercube) is *supposed* to look. If you're interested, there are several videos online that you can watch about the *Hypercube* and I encourage you to look one or two up in order to drive home the point.

If you watched some videos, you will notice that it is impossible to explain exactly what the Hypercube looks like. There are no drawings of how it looks because we cannot draw, see, communicate or visualize in four dimensions. We can describe its building blocks, or how its shadow would look like in three dimensions, or how its cross-section would look like as it travelled through a three-dimensional world. But what we cannot do is describe or visualize what this conceptual shape looks like in its original form in four-dimensions. The real you, using intelligence and reasoning, can figure out that this shape exists, and that it is made of 8 cubes (see the trend above of *two* dots, *four* lines, *six* squares...so the next dimensional shape must have *eight* cubes). But your animal mind cannot instinctively understand or visualize it. Your body's mind simply cannot keep up with your rational intelligent mind's abstract capacities.

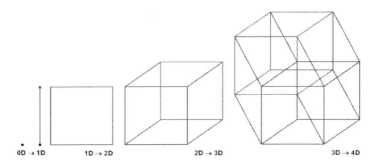

0D → 1D   1D → 2D   2D → 3D   3D → 4D

A purple duck is just as elusive as a Tesseract, for neither exists in our present world or dimension, nor has any human being ever seen a purple duck (any sober human being at least). But, even though your vessel's brain cannot possibly visualize a hypercube, it can definitely visualize a purple duck. Why is that? The difference is the hypercube exists in a dimension that your body's mind can never conceptualise, and so it cannot make-up what it cannot perceive. But a purple duck…well your animal mind knows what purple is, and what a duck is and so with the help of your intelligent mind's imagination, the body's mind can easily visualize the two together. This would be a simple combination of things your body's mind has already observed seen in this temporal world, so you can superimpose them (in other words the mind can photo shop two things that it has already seen together to make something it has never seen). But a hypercube, like your true self (the conscious rational intelligent mind that lives in this vessel's brain) has no representation in our physical world or its three-dimension.

The hypercube is one simple example of what math and science have uncovered, conceptually, that our animal minds simply don't understand. Here's another quick example: Do a quick survey of the people around you. Even today, a whole 122 years after the theory of time dilation was predicted, your average person (your humble author included) cannot fathom how a run-of-the-mill watch (the same one you might have on your arm – digital or mechanical) will ACTUALLY run faster at higher altitudes or velocities. Gravitational time is a proven theorem that has been both postulated by scientists (such as in Einstein's theory of relativity) and observed through experiments (both here on earth and in space)[16]. Yet it is still difficult for us to wrap our instinctive minds around it. I mean a watch is a watch! How can it possibly speed up because it's on top of a building or mountain or is travelling faster (say in a car or a plane) than another identical watch?! This just does not make sense to us instinctively because our sensory organs experience time as a unidirectional constant. Yet we can understand how and why this is true through the language of mathematics. This difference in capacities of perception vs conception is a result of the duality within (i.e. the animal mind with its primitive thoughts and perceptions vs your rational intelligent mind with its conceptual capabilities).

---

[16] *The theory of time dilation was first predicted by Larmor in 1897. This work then led to theories in Lorenz transformation that was then expanded upon by Albert Einstein in his work on Equivalence principle in 1907. Finally, the crescendo of all this research was reached when in 1917 Einstein postulated his famous Theory of Relativity. These theories were all proven in 1925 through observations by W.S. Adams (and many more that followed), and since then many demonstrations (with atomic clocks) have been made as well to prove the accuracy of Einstein's theories. Today we know for a fact that Newton's gravitational "laws" are in reality incorrect, and that Einstein's Theory of Relativity is a much better predictor of objects' movements in gravitational fields. We still teach Newton's Laws in school, however, because it is accurate beyond an observable margin of error when it comes to large objects, and it is orders of magnitude simpler than the Theory of Relativity.*

Before we go further down this rabbit hole of the "split minds" within you, let us first clarify one question: Why do we refer to your rational side (the consciousness within) as the "real you", as opposed to your instinctive "autopilot" that we know is more often active and in charge? Well, who is reading these words right now? It is not the part of you that just wants to eat (sustain itself), sleep (rest and recuperate), fornicate (propagation of the species), etc. Pretty much all other life forms that we know of do these things to a varying degree or another. Instead, the part of you that is reading this and wants to learn is the higher level of thought: Your rational mind.

Your body, which is your vessel, is an animal. It is reactive to its environment through pre-coded feelings and chemical/hormonal/electrical responses. It is a blind slave to its senses. The rational mind, on the other hand, is emotionless and feels no pleasure. It seeks only equanimity. Your animal mind is purely concerned with keeping itself functional and alive. Your rational ordinary (as in emotionless) mind is connected to the human community and wants to do good in this world for others. It knows right from wrong. This is why you feel joy when you help an old lady cross the street, or hold the door for someone, or simply smile and say "hello" to a stranger.

"But irrational animals share with man many of the same faculties. And so for the beasts it is enough to eat, drink, sleep, breed and do whatever else it is that satisfies members of their kind. But for us who have been given the faculty of understanding, this is not enough. Unless we act appropriately, methodically, and in line with our nature and constitution, we will fall short of our proper purpose."

- Epictetus

Animals, including our own bodies, can be found everywhere in nature. However, the consciousness we have is a unique gift to human beings only (at least as far as we have observed to date[17]). This special and unique gift (whether it is given by the gods, is pure chance, or is a being of its own that manifests itself in us) is what connects all humans beings across time, borders, race,

---

[17] *Technically, we cannot be certain that animals do not have a consciousness, as we cannot communicate with them. Even though most people would agree that animals do not possess consciousness to the same degree as do humans, we must admit that this is based on assumptions made from observations of their behaviours. Moreover, some animals have demonstrated the capacity for self-awareness (gorillas) and some have demonstrated the capacity for rational thought (e.g. a fox that will gnaw off its limb to get out of a trap and survive). Given that there is no agreed upon definition of consciousness, the discussion of whether animals have a consciousness or not becomes even more ambiguous. For the purposes of this book, however, this question becomes irrelevant. It matters not whether other animals have a consciousness. It only matters that we focus on cultivating our own to achieve a tranquil life.*

social class, etc. All 7.6 billion of us share this unique gift today. All 100 billion Homo Sapiens who ever roamed the world following the Cognitive Revolution shared this unique gift. We may live in large groups (such as cities) and form and participate in local *Human Societies*, but this exclusive gift that we share with our brothers and sisters is what connects us in the special and exclusive realm of the *Human Community*. This connection is a significant part of our nature and thus forms part of our natural behaviour. This connection, and this gift, is what makes the rational ordinary mind the "real-you."

> "Revere the faculty that produces opinion. This faculty determines whether there shall exist in your ruling part any opinion inconsistent with nature and this faculty promises freedom from hasty judgment, friendship towards men and obedience to the gods."
>
> -   Marcus Aurelius

We could all benefit from Socrates' dictum "Know Thyself." I'm sure you know endless amounts of trivia about yourself, like when you had your first kiss, or how much savings you have in the bank, or your body's height and weight, or the last time you had a bowel movement. But what do you truly know about your real self? The real self that you have never seen in a mirror?

We go through life setting goals that we believe we should be pursuing (whether it be an athletic accomplishment, having the dream job, buying a house, etc.). Sometimes we get lucky and accomplish these goals...but then still find ourselves asking the questions: Who am I? What's important to me? What do I truly need? Most of us go through life without ever knowing much about our real selves, let alone recognizing who we truly are. But once you know who you truly are and are aware of this inner discourse, the conversation (or debate) between your own mind and your body's mind becomes just a little more manageable and clearer, and life becomes a little more tranquil and enjoyable.

"Those who enjoy life are wiser than those who employ life."

- Lao Tzu

8 RECOGNIZING WHO IS IN CONTROL

Try this quick thought experiment and do it as honestly and objectively as you can: Linda is thirty-one years old, single, outspoken, and very bright. She majored in philosophy. As a student, she was deeply concerned with issues of discrimination and social justice, and also participated in antinuclear demonstrations. Rank the following in likelihood of possible scenarios:

- Linda is a teacher in elementary school.
- Linda works in a bookstore and takes yoga classes.
- Linda is active in the feminist movement.
- Linda is a psychiatric social worker.
- Linda is a member of the League of Women Voters.
- Linda is a bank teller.
- Linda is an insurance salesperson.

- Linda is a bank teller and is active in the feminist movement.

When you ranked the above, which was more likely?

- Linda is a bank teller.
- Linda is a bank teller and is active in the feminist movement.

As far as managing the two voices within are concerned, it has been made clear in previous chapters that one cannot simply turn off the animal mind and call it a day. The duality, therefore, must be managed in a more holistic way with the ultimate goal of ensuring that both voices are present (in your inner discourse) and that the animal body (who is prone to take control without notice), is not blindly steering the ship. The animal mind runs the show solo too often. For example, when you act out of character or act irrationally (while emotional), only to regret your choice of actions after the fact, it is an example of when your animal mind is running the show alone. When you are calm (after the fact) and reflect on your own actions with your rational ordinary mind and ask yourself *"What was I thinking?"* then your rational mind is back in the driver's seat.

We know that biologically speaking, the brain, along with the intestines, use up the most amount of energy. In fact, anthropological evidence suggests that up until fairly recently in our evolution the intestines used to be the largest consumer of calories in the animal body to get the necessary nutrients from the ingested food. About 800,000 years ago, fire was domesticated by the human species, and by about 300,000 ago fire was being used on a daily basis. This made the food our ancestors ate more easily digestible (and therefore easier to extract nutrients from). This in turn led to a significant reduction in the length of the intestinal tract, thus greatly reducing its caloric requirements in extracting the required nutrients from the ingested food. This reduction in energy consumption was directly related to the increase in brain sizes as the calories were now freed-up to feed a bigger brain[18]. So regularly cooking our food, helped our ancestors' brains grow due to reduced lengths in intestines, and ultimately was a significant contributor to the Cognitive revolution (thanks fire!). As a result of this transformation, today the human brain is the single most energy dependent organ in our body, accounting for up to 20% of the entire daily caloric use.

Why is all this pertinent? Simple: Thinking requires the use of the brain, which is why thinking is hard and exhausting! Of course, anyone who has ever written an exam already knows this. Biologically and anthropologically speaking, we have empirical evidence to show that thinking uses a LOT of resources. So, you should not be insulted to learn that you are lazy. The real you (your rational intelligent mind) is, just like anything else in nature, lazy. Nature is known for following the path of least resistance. As far as organic life is concerned, it seeks the most return for the output of energy. Nature (including you) is efficient. It is a

---

[18] *Some anthropologists believe that early humans cooking before eating their food might have been a significant factor leading to the evolution of Homo Sapiens.*

simple game of math: Get back as much as you can in return for the minimum amount of effort (i.e. energy output) so as to improve your chances of continuity.

Making moral and rational decisions about everything all day long would be exhausting to say the least. Moreover, it would quite literally bring your life to a grinding halt due to overthinking. This is where your "autopilot" system comes into play (as discussed in chapter 4) and we rely on it most of the time. In modern day psychology, these split-second auto pilot decisions are referred to as heuristics. These heuristics can lead to various errors, such as availability, representativeness, conjunction, affect, anchoring and adjustment fallacies (amongst others). But essentially a heuristic can be summarized as a simple "short-cut" procedure that helps the "autopilot" attain adequate, though often imperfect, answers to the questions you face.

Heuristics simplify our lives by creating a world that is much tidier than reality (as in simpler, where everything makes sense). Your lazy rational intelligent mind wants to conserve energy, so it follows the path of least resistance. As such, it often endorses the oversimplified heuristic answers that your body's mind puts forth (rationalization), without much scrutiny of whether it is truly the right decision or appropriate to the given context and situation.

"The prime principle then in man's constitution is the social. And the second is not to yield to the persuasions of the body, for it is the peculiar office of the rational and intelligent motion to circumscribe itself, and never to be overpowered either by the motion of the senses or of the appetites, for both are animal; but the intelligent motion claims superiority and does not permit itself to be overpowered by others."

- Marcus Aurelius

As intelligent as we are, it can be difficult to accept that we get lazy and believe oversimplified and blatantly wrong answers and interpretations of our world. This is especially difficult to accept when it happens while being "duped" by our animal mind into believing that we are using our rational minds in making intelligent decisions. Modern psychologists study this problem in depth to understand it better and offer solutions to mitigate it. A famous experiment to help study this phenomenon is the Linda experiment, which was first conducted by Amos Tversky and Daniel Kahneman.

At the beginning of the chapter. you were presented with a question, and if you answered it like most of the respondents, you ranked Linda being a bank teller *and* being active in the feminist movement as being more probable than her *just* being a bank teller. If so, you were wrong even though you are probably convinced that you were making a reasonable and intelligent assessment. Your mind simply took the path of least resistance.

Your logical mind took the lazy way out and relied on your instinctive "autopilot" and its heuristic. The culprit in this case was the conjunction fallacy. The probability of two events occurring together (in conjunction) are always less or equal to the probability of either one occurring alone. All bank tellers that are active in the feminist movement are (still) bank tellers. However, not all bank tellers are active in the feminist movement. Therefore, from a purely statistical standpoint, Linda is more likely to be a bank teller, even though her profile sounds more "fitting" of a bank teller who is also active in the feminist movement. This profile "fit", however, does not change the statistical facts. Even if she is active in the feminist movement, she is still a bank teller. When you take a step back and think about it (as you now engage your logical mind), you understand the simple statistical facts and realize that you unwillingly replaced the question of "which is she more likely to be" with the simpler question of "which role does her profile fit better." Up until a few minutes ago, however, you were convinced that you answered the question with your rational intelligent mind, and not your "autopilot" with its heuristics.

Was this a play on words? A trick? No, it was not. The wording was clear from the beginning. The fault is your lazy rational mind relying on the "autopilot" of your body's primitive mind that made a profile judgment (because it was easier) instead of making an objective statistical evaluation of probabilities. As you went through the list of possibilities, almost assuredly you were tying each potential scenario to Linda's profile, instead of evaluating statistically the likelihood of each scenario being true.

For example, when comparing the probability between her being a social worker vs insurance broker, you probably did not stop to consider the effect of the total number of available jobs in the market (e.g. if there are 10,000 insurance salespersons to every 1 psychiatric social worker, then even if the profile fits the social worker role better, she is statistically more likely to be an insurance broker…we all need paychecks). There are many other objective statistical factors you never considered in your evaluation of Linda and the listed scenarios. This clearly was not your rational intelligent mind at work.

This example is a simple demonstration of how quickly, easily, often and (most alarming) stealthily the "autopilot" will take over, while giving you a sense of still being in control *("You're in charge buddy, all is good, don't worry!")*. You were confident that your answer above was logical. However, confidence is a mere feeling which reflects the coherence of information *("it makes sense in my mind")* and the cognitive ease of processing it *("in my world picture this not only makes sense but fits so perfectly that it must be true!")*.

Heuristics are not all bad. For the most part they can be useful and are often necessary. Lest we forget, being alert all the time would be exhausting. But the point and lesson here is that the heuristics operate under the clandestine pretense of you being in control with your rational logical and intelligent mind. We must be aware of this to be vigilant against it when necessary.

Modern day research shows time and time again that the "autopilot" of the primitive mind (the animal mind) and our faculty of deliberate thought (the real you) draw on the same limited budget of resources and energy. People avoid cognitive load/strain when possible (nature is lazy and takes the path of least resistance), so we fall back on the "autopilot." Ever drive somewhere, get to your destination, and realize you were never really focused on the drive itself when you got there? This is because "you" were not driving. "You" were thinking about the office, or chores, or the weekend, etc. while the "autopilot" (animal mind) was going through the motions of driving the same route you drive every day.

Keith Stanovich in his book "Rationality and the Reflective Mind" draws a sharp distinction between the two minds. The "real you" is algorithmic, slow thinking, demanding, computational and analytical. This is your faculty of reason, your rational ordinary and intelligent mind. When engaged, the algorithmic mind cannot be irrational. So, the caveat here is to have the capacity to engage it when necessary, and not rely on heuristics. Therefore, the goal (and challenge) is to try and be aware of who is in control, and to try (as much as possible) to engage the rational ordinary mind when the circumstances demand it. You must therefore get in the habit of asking yourself the question: Who is in control?

9 LOOK BEYOND THE PATTERNS. EMBRACE THE DIFFERENT

By now you are getting an understanding of how different the two minds are and how distinctly they both think and operate. The Linda experiment is a simple demonstration of how quickly the body's mind (or animal mind) can take over and fool you with the illusion that "you" are in control, when the "real you" is blissfully ignorant in the background. Lucky for you, your consciousness ultimately has the option to see reality for what it is, by recognizing who is in control, and by engaging your higher capacities for thought…if you so choose.

We are pattern seekers. Our animal minds prefer to believe in a simple and coherent world. Instinctively, we do not like surprises and find comfort in familiar patterns. When we detect what appears to be a pattern or regularity, we quickly reject the idea that the process is truly random (i.e. we do not expect to see patterns produced by a random process). This is part of the general vigilance that we have inherited from our ancestors. We are on the lookout for the possibility that our safe, regular and unchanging environment has in fact changed and might harbour a new threat. If something appears random or out of place, it may be a lion approaching. So, the ancestor that spotted the difference and began running sooner made it further than the ones who were indifferent to change and thus lived longer to pass on their genes, which you now possess.

A simplified version of this thought process is that if you are happily alive with the way things are right now, then instinctively you do not want things to change, as the current state of affairs equals remaining alive. Instinctively, we do not like that which does not fit in the regular sequence of your daily events. We love our routines[19].

Whoever you are and whatever type of life you live, you instinctively and effortlessly detect when things change. How do you feel when you are at home at night, watching your TV series that you binge on, sitting in the same seat you usually sit in...and all of a sudden, your doorbell rings? Or your phone rings? Or something happens like a noise right outside your house? Or you believe to have seen something move and stare at that spot of the perceived anomaly with anxiety and heightened senses? How would you feel?

---

[19] *This does not mean we live monotonous and boring lives. If you are a thrill seeker, your daily activities will consist of adrenaline-pumping events. So, doing something more "boring" would be the uncomfortable change from the routine for the adrenaline junkie.*

This is an example of the instinct you have inherited regarding the dislike of a change in your environment. A change, especially an unexpected one, is automatically perceived as a threat. This potentially crippling inheritance of your body's mind is one of many ways in which our inherent pessimism manifests itself. As human beings we are inherently pessimistic (e.g. the mind gives priority to bad news). And as already outlined, anthropologically speaking, pessimism is a built-in and very necessary survival mechanism that helped our species get to where we are today. However, in today's modern world it is no longer all that necessary. Unfortunately, no matter how hopeful we may try to be on the surface or try and have a positive disposition, deep down most of us will make a pessimistic prediction more often than not when it is left up to the "autopilot."

> "The aim of our studies should be to direct the mind with a view to forming true and sound judgments about whatever comes before it. A person should consider how to increase the natural light of his reason, in order that his intellect should show his will what decisions it ought to make."
>
> - René Descartes

The ancient Stoic philosophers recognized this inherent weakness our animal minds possesses and spent a lot of time on trying to mitigate it through a mental exercise called *Premeditatio Malorum* ("premeditation of evils"). It consists of consciously thinking about what bad/terrible thing could or will realistically happen. Through repetitive meditation on this possible scenario, one can be prepared to better accept it with equanimity, should it come to fruition. The alternative would be losing yourself over a "negative" event or (worse) worrying about a "negative" event before it even happens (regardless of whether it even happens). Best to simply accept that it *can* happen. This way you can be better prepared if it does come to pass, and more importantly, *appreciate what you have today* as opposed to living with the *worry of losing it.*

> "When a man kisses his child, says Epictetus, he should whisper to himself, 'tomorrow perchance you will die.' "
>
> - Marcus Aurelius

As a parent and a Stoic practitioner, I still can't bring myself to very realistically accept the possibility of the death of my children. Children tragically die young all the time all over the world. This is a fact of life, and I'm no different than any of the parents who have had to bury their child. I know this to be a possible (though not probable) scenario, yet even after years of practice, I still find myself getting melancholy, teary eyed, and physically uncomfortable when I try and visualize and accept the chance of one of them dying from natural causes or being hit by a car, or from one of hundreds of thousands of other ways they can die (even as I write this my mind is screaming *"Touch wood! Touch wood!"*).

This very real risk of a devastating change in my life is a topic that my rational mind knows I should accept and be mentally prepared for. If such a tragedy should occur, I will still have other dependents who rely on me and need me to be at my best. As such, being mentally prepared for such a change makes logical sense to my rational mind. And due to my emotional and physical reaction, I find it very difficult to do so.

The point, of course, is not to constantly think about and drown in depressing thoughts of all that may go wrong and live in misery. The goal is to just be able to accept (really accept) what *can* go wrong, so as to be able to appreciate what we have now, and to be able to deal with events as they happen in a "matter-of-fact" fashion. The alternative is to be stuck in the spiral of *"this is unfair, why did it happen to me, life sucks!"* I'm sure you can think of more than a few examples of devastating events in your life. At the time they may have felt almost surreal and unfair (emotional response). Today, you can look back and see that it was merely a possible event that came to fruition. In other words, no matter how bad the event, you can accept that it just happened…this was not a conspiracy on the part of the universe against you. It just is. This would be the rational intelligent response.

> "Let death and exile, and all other things which appear terrible be daily before your eyes, but chiefly death, and you will never entertain any abject thought, nor too eagerly covet anything."
>
> -   Epictetus

We hate change, and flat out ignore the really big and uncomfortable ones (like the death of a loved one) as even being possibilities. The biggest changes you will be faced with in your lifetime relate to your own existential shortcomings. Your body's mind tends to make your rational mind ignore two important facts of life: your mortality and your insignificance. Death is the ultimate change. We have an irrational fear of acknowledging our own mortality. Our death is uncomfortable to think about, but lest we forget is a certainty. We ignore it and pretend it is not going to happen for a long time (long enough that we don't even have to consider it). This irrational fear, however, is just that: irrational. Fearing or ignoring something that is 100% guaranteed to happen is at best an extreme form of ignorance, and at worse insanity in denial of reality.

The ancient Stoics were known to keep the idea of death very close to their hearts: *Memento Mori* (Remember death). This was not due to some morbid sense of humor, but it had two very concrete objectives. Firstly, it was a reminder to not fear their own or their loved one's deaths. Death is bound to happen so best to accept it and be prepared for it, as opposed to losing one's mind from feeling like the most improbable unfair injustice just happened. The second and more impactful purpose of this mantra, was to constantly remind themselves of the gift of time. They recognized the importance of being mindful of the true value of their very limited and most precious resource: their consciousness in the here and now (i.e. life & time).

> "People are frugal in guarding their personal property; but as soon as it comes to squandering time they are most wasteful of the one thing in which it is right to be stingy."
>
> -   Lucius Annaeus Seneca

How many more "Here and Nows" are there left in your life? Wouldn't you rather be aware of this (at first scary, but then liberating) fact, to then better manage and spend your time? If you had a wallet stuffed with a finite amount of money, wouldn't you rather spend every dollar wisely? Sure, it may be stuffed with green bills now, but knowing full well that it *will* run out one day would you spend it frivolously and without paying any attention? Would you waste it all on trivialities until you reach in for one more dollar bill one day and come up empty handed?

> "It is not that we have so little time but that we waste so much of it...The life we receive is not short but we make it so; we are not ill provided but use what we have wastefully."
>
> -   Lucius Annaeus Seneca

The part of you that understands the logic behind all this is your rational mind. The part that feels uncomfortable for some reason even though you can't quite put your finger on why that is, is the primitive mind's animal instincts of survival. It does not want to even consider your own mortality. But if your rational mind ignores these instinctive emotions and fears, it clearly and easily understands that reflecting on your own mortality in a disciplined meditating approach over time will have the opposite effect than what your "gut instinct" tells you. That is, instead of sadness and melancholy, you would cultivate invigoration and motivation to spend your precious time more wisely, as opposed to being distracted in the pursuit of worldly goods and sensory pleasures.

"Think of the life you have lived until now as over and, as a dead man, see what's left as a bonus and live it according to Nature. Love the hand that fate deals you and play it as your own, for what could be more fitting?"

- Marcus Aurelius

The other big change (in paradigm) we ignore is coming to terms with our insignificance (as in realizing we're not special). As children, we are recounted wonderful fairy tales that tell us we're special and deserve everything we desire in life. Even if others suffer, we will still be benefactors of good fortune as long as we are nice (good guys always win and we're the good guys!). However, in the cosmic scale of things – or even in the human history scale of things – it is hard to argue that we are individually significant or special in anyway. You are 0.000000001% [20] of all human beings who have ever existed. You will live (maybe) to occupy 0.00000072% [21] of time that has existed in the known universe. In all of observable space (and we know there is much much more of it beyond our detection) you occupy only 4.13% x 10^{-50} [22] of matter in the universe. Your animal mind, however,

---

[20] *100 billion human beings have walked the earth so far, so individually neither one of us is special.*

[21] *Assuming you will live 100 years, the observable universe is 13.8 billion years old. You occupy a miniscule point in (known) time.*

[22] *Our best estimate is that the universe contains 1.5 x 10^{53} kg of matter, and your average adult human today (in the world, not North America only) weighs 62 kg. Any which way you look at it, we are tiny specs in both time and space.*

is focused only on its own survival, so it is thinking "me, me, me...I'm special."

We like to think we are the central character of the only story in history that matters. But the simple and logical (if you can remain emotionless) truth is that there is a gaping difference between being "special" and being "unique." We can all agree that we are unique individuals as we are all different in our own ways. But what makes you more special or more important than any other of the other 100 billion human beings to have ever existed on this planet? Or the 7.6 billion that exist today? What gives you more importance or rights over anyone else?

> "What other course remains for men but that which Socrates took when asked to what country he belonged, never to say 'I am an Athenian,' or 'I am a Corinthian,' but 'I am a citizen of the universe.'"
>
> - Epictetus

10 FURTHER DOWN THE RABBIT HOLE...IS ANY OF IT REAL?

You are reading this book, right? You are holding it...it is in your hands...it is a real thing that you are touching, feeling and seeing. Yet it is merely a collection of atoms, which are 99.99% empty space, so it isn't actually there. It exists as far as your mind perceives is to be there. You may think your surroundings are made of objects the way you see them, but objects only exist as far as they are perceived in your mind. In fact, there is a whole branch of philosophy dedicated to the study of reality existing only in your mind, called Absolute Idealism[23]. It asserts that nothing exists other than the individual consciousness and what

---

[23]*Absolute Idealism is a philosophical theory chiefly associated with G.W.F. Hegel. It means that the finite world is a reflection of mind, which alone is the only truly real thing. The common everyday world of things is not the world as it really is but merely appears to be as such in the self-conscious mind.*

it imagines or hallucinates in its thoughts. At first light, this sounds a bit absurd. It would mean that everything you "see" only exists in your mind and is not actually "there" in front of you. But think about the dreams you have. Do they not seem real when you are in them? Do you not touch and interact with things and people in your dreams? And is there any way you can be absolutely sure that what you see really exists beyond the way you "see" it in your mind and imagination? There truly is no way to verify anything or be sure about anything beyond your own thoughts' existence. René Descartes summarized this uncomfortable truth in his axiom *Cogito Ergo Sum* (I think therefore I am). "You" are thinking, so you know "you" (the real you, as in the rational intelligent consciousness) exist. But beyond that, how do you know that the book you are holding actually exists outside of your mind? Or that your hands that are holding it exist? Or the rest of the world?

All objects outside of the mind (including one's own body), then, are subjective to the subject observing them. This is a topic that can get very heavy and foggy very fast. Many psychologists and philosophers explore the realm of "reality," what it is, what it can be and what we can be sure about. As interesting as the topic can be, however, it is outside the scope of our work here. As far as your search for a tranquil life is concerned, it will suffice to simply recognize that what you think is in front of you, is in fact not in front of you *exactly the way you think it is*. For arguments sake let's just agree that the world around us does exist. You still only see "things" as an internal projection. This becomes very relevant, as you quickly realize what you think is in your hands right now, is presented to the real you (your rational intelligent mind) not the way it objectively exists outside your mind, but the way your animal body perceives it and projects it to you internally using its sensory organs. Your consciousness lives inside this vessel and can only interact with the outside world through this vessel. So, whatever you see and observe to be out there gets warped as it is projected inwards through the sensory organs and central nervous system of the vessel. This is yet another example of how your animal mind and higher faculty of reason have different paradigms in which they operate.

"First impressions are always unreliable."

-   Franz Kafka

I can't stress enough the gravity of recognizing that your outside world is being warped as you "observe" it internally with your real self. Your "view" of the world is fatally flawed from the moment you observe it. You can never be sure that what you "see" or "observe" externally is actually objectively the way it is. Here's a simple real-life example. As a color-blind person, people ask me all the time what colors I see and how they look to me. I usually answer this question with a question of my own: What colors do *you* see and how can you be sure you see them the same way someone else does? Think about it. You look at a banana, your eyes absorb the light waves that bounce off of it, the optical nerves translate this into an image in your brain, and your mind goes *"yes this is yellow, a yellow banana…same shade as a raincoat or the sun or SpongeBob!"* In your mind's projection (internally) you have an image and definition of what yellow is and can point at everything that is yellow. But can you describe yellow? You can look at a banana with someone else, and you will both agree that it is a color that you both refer to as yellow. You also will agree that raincoats, the sun and SpongeBob are a color you refer to as yellow. But how do you know they see yellow the same way you do in their own mind's projection? How do you know that what you perceive as yellow in your mind is not the equivalent of what someone else sees as orange? Or another as red or purple? You would both always point at the objects with the color labeled "yellow" and agree that they are "yellow." But you can never be sure what you "see" is the same as what someone else does.

The big takeaway here is that as you observe the world you only see what is projected internally through the biases of the tools that your animal vessel possesses. This includes flaws in its sensory tools, its own (instinctive) assumptions and emotions, and the way all this is put together in a type of hallucination and movie inside your brain that is then finally projected to the *real you*.

> "What Is the cause of assenting to anything? The fact that it appears to be true. It is not possible then to assent to that which appears not to be true. Why? Because this is the nature of the understanding, to incline to the true, to be dissatisfied with the false, and in matters uncertain to withhold assent."
>
> - Epictetus

It is not the goal of this book to explore possible realms of reality from a philosophical perspective. This rabbit hole has no conceivable end. One can spend a lifetime exploring this without coming up with any real answers. I don't know about you, but I don't have that many heart beats left to spare on exploring such academic ideas before I learn to live a tranquil life. However, it's still good information that can be used to our advantage in learning to live a better life. Taking in new information to better yourself is your duty to yourself. So if we know that things external to your my mind can only be viewed by your rational intelligent mind as far as they are projected internally to you by the animal vessel in a flawed and inaccurate manner, the question is this: How can you use this information to live a better and more tranquil life?

"Don't tell yourself anything more than what the initial impressions report...A cucumber is bitter, 'Throw it away' ...This is enough. Do not add 'And why were such things made in the world?' For you will be ridiculed by a man who is acquainted with nature, as you would be ridiculed by a carpenter and shoemaker if you found fault because you saw in their workshop shavings and cuttings from the things they make."

- Marcus Aurelius

It is easier to care less about the things external to your mind's thoughts when you realize that all such "externals" (people, objects, events) are not the full picture of what you think you see...or rather that they are misrepresentations. Those "things" which you are presented as being "good" or "bad" are not the way they appear to be at first light. The moment impressions are presented to you internally, they are misrepresentations at best, or flat out lies at worst. So, when you see that annoying driver cutting you off in traffic, due to intuitive reactions of the "autopilot" you will be convinced the individual in the other car is selfish and a soulless pig with no morals or love of others. Under calm and ordinary circumstances, however, your rational mind can admit to a reality that is simply factual and without biases of judgments: There is a car...with a driver...that cut in your lane. Period. Pure factual statements. Anything more (e.g. the driver is a pig, is selfish, the act was "bad" and a crime against nature!) are all additional *value judgments* that were tacked on in a guerilla like fashion by your animal mind's instincts, without you ever having a chance to even contemplate if said judgments are in fact true.

> "When we have meat before us and such eatables, we receive the impression that this is the dead body of a fish, and this is the dead body of a bird or of a pig; and again, that this fine wine is only a little grape juice, and this purple robe some sheep's wool dyed with the blood of a shellfish or, in the matter of sexual intercourse, that it is merely rubbing private parts together and the spasmodic expulsion of semen: such then are these impressions, and they reach the things themselves and penetrate them, and so we see the things as they truly are."
>
> - Marcus Aurelius

You would not give advice to someone without having all the information you could. Or if you were a judge, you would not render a verdict without having all the facts, right? So why have an opinion on your surroundings, if you cannot objectively perceive all that is? Why give advice (or assessment/judgments of a "thing") to yourself if you do not have all the information? Why render a verdict on your "view" of things without having all the facts?

> "When we intend to judge weights, we do not judge by guess: where we intend to judge of straight and crooked, we do not judge by guess. In all cases where it is our interest to know what is true in any matter, never will any man among us do anything by guess. But in things which depend on the first and the only cause of doing right or wrong, of happiness or unhappiness, of being fortunate or unfortunate, there only we are inconsiderate and rash. There is nothing like scales, nothing like a rule: but some appearance is presented, and straightaway I act according to it...And what is the name of those who follow every appearance? They are called madmen."
>
> -   Epictetus

Your body's primitive animal mind is limited in its view of the world and capabilities of perception, so it will naturally have unduly quick opinions based on partial information and will want to hastily act on them. This is a built-in function that may have been necessary in the past but the real you no longer needs this rash response mechanism, especially not in today's modern world. You have the choice, thanks to your rational ordinary mind's awareness, to see beyond that which is immediately presented. You have the choice to consciously try to avoid making an unduly quick and rash opinion based on the limited information your body's mind has gathered and warped for your (internal) viewing pleasure.

> "Don't let the force of an impression when it first hits you knock you off your feet; just say to it, 'Hold on a moment; let me see who you are and what you represent. Let me put you to the test' "
>
> -   Epictetus

That driver that cut you off did not do what they did because they were a bad person or decided to do bad on to you. They may have had a very legitimate reason for behaving the way they did. Maybe they were in a rush to get to a hospital, or had an urgency of some sort, etc....Even if they did not have a legitimate reason (i.e. they were just straight up selfish) do you have to get upset? What is done is done, and it is in the past already. Anything you do past that point is your decision and choice, not someone else's doing. You (the real you) has a choice to see the bigger picture beyond the limited scope of the warped inward representations and simply forgive.

ANDERSON SILVER

"There are certain people who act out of the animal mind. When someone hits them, they want to hit back, retaliate. With our human brain, we can think, 'If I hit back, what use will it be in the long-term?' ...The cause of someone hitting us was ultimately their anger, their ignorance, their short-sightedness, their narrow-mindedness. So that brings a sense of concern, and we can feel sorry for these people. So, it is totally wrong to say that practice of tolerance and practice of forgiveness are signs of weakness...Those who say forgiving is a sign of weakness haven't tried it."

- Dalai Lama

You have committed wrongdoings in the past, for you are human and we all make mistakes. But you haven't done them with the specific inclination to be evil, did you? You are not even aware of most wrongdoings you make, as they are incidental, unintentional and collateral. If you can be honest with yourself, then you know you have done things in the past that you wish you hadn't and you also recognize that you most assuredly did many wrong things, impacting others negatively that you are not even aware of. Does this mean you are a bad person? No, they were unintentional or incidental. But not recognizing that the actions of others also fall into this same category, would be a crime against the rest of humanity. Why do you get to inconvenience others by mistake and seek forgiveness, if you don't allow others the same latitude? No matter how difficult, or how unfairly treated the animal mind and body will want you to feel, you must try and keep the rational mind active and in the

87

"conversation." This is how you can remain objective and forgive, as opposed to responding with emotions and have knee-jerk reactions.

> "Where is the harm or the strangeness in the boor acting like a boor? See whether you are not yourself the more to blame in not expecting that he would err in such a way. For you had means given you by your reason to suppose that it was likely that he would commit this error, and yet you have forgotten and are amazed that he has erred...Wherein have you been injured? For you will find that no one among those against whom you are irritated has done anything by which your mind could be made worse; but that which is evil to you and harmful has its foundations only in the mind."
>
> - Marcus Aurelius

Being forgiving no matter the circumstances would be as easy as flipping a light switch if you could function *only* within the confines of your rational ordinary mind. But the fact is that your rational ordinary mind lives and exists within the framework of this animal vessel that has its own primitive instincts, emotions and reactions. We cannot shut it off, and we cannot (yet) exist outside of it. We must therefore live with it. So, the key is to remember that you live *with it*...you are *not it*.

> "An eye for an eye will leave the whole world blind."
>
> - Archbishop Desmond Tutu

The primitive instincts that make up your body and its emotions are reactive by nature (like most in the animal kingdom). Conversely, your capacity for reason is proactive. The real you can conceptualize thoughts and think in the abstract. You (the real rational you) can conceptualize a purple duck and what it might look like. Your animal mind cannot. Your animal mind is primitive, but what it lacks in higher faculties, it makes up in sheer noise and volume.

The vessel's mind likes taking up space in your inner dialogue to the point of being the only voice there. So, your primary goal is to be aware of this extra tool you have (that is your rational intelligent mind), and to make sure it does not get lost and forgotten behind the clamour of the body's animal mind in your inner dialogue. You cannot shut off the animal mind, but you can ensure it is not taking the driver's seat of your ruling faculty all for itself. You have a magnificent gift that is your consciousness and this higher rational faculty within you. So, make sure it is involved in your inner dialogue, debating with the vessel's primitive mind. This is the very least you can and should do.

> "Animals without eyes know only by touch what is immediately present to them in space, from what comes in contact with them. Animals that see, on the other hand, know a wide sphere of what is near and distant. In the same way, the absence of reason restricts the animals to representations of perception immediately present to them in time, in other words to real objects. We, on the

other hand, by virtue of knowledge in the abstract, comprehend not only the narrow and actual present, but also the whole past and future together with the wide realm of possibility. We survey life freely in all directions, far beyond what is present and actual. Thus, what the eye is in space and for sensuous knowledge, reason is, to a certain extent, in time and for inner knowledge."

- Arthur Schopenhauer

11 SPIRITUALITY: IT'S A THING AND YOU SHOULD DO IT

"Adolf Hitler and Albert Einstein were essentially the same." If one were to truly believe there is nothing more to us human beings beyond the physical representation that is "the body," then this statement would be undeniably and logically correct. If one were to look at an infant Hitler and an Einstein toddler, you would not see much of a difference. Born 10 years and 250 km apart, the two were fairly identical physical specimens. Deoxyribonucleic acid (DNA) is the code that maps physical properties of the carbon-based lifeforms on the planet. If one were to look at their DNA, Hitler and Einstein's DNA would have been less than 0.01% apart (which is the case between any two human beings from any point on the planet). They both had two legs, two arms, two eyes, one mouth, a nose, digestive systems and physical necessities that were identical. Yet, I would be hard pressed to find anyone who would agree that they were essentially the same person.

It is clear that there is "something more" over and above the physical representation that is our bodies. Human beings have known this far before we settled down to farm. We know this from religious and spiritual artifacts that have been found dating back almost 35,000 years[24]. Note that this predates the agricultural revolution (about 10,000 years ago) and comes after the Cognitive revolution (about 70,000 years ago). During this time there has been little debate over whether there *is* "something more" over and above the physical but only differing opinions on what it actually is, where it came from and where it's going. On one side of the spectrum the most avid atheist cannot deny that there is something within us that exists without physical properties, even if it is merely electrical signals shooting around in our brain (the thinky bits that would have made Hitler and Einstein very different.). It does not mean that it was put there by a god; it does not mean it goes somewhere after death, but there exists this consciousness within us that is not a tangible physical thing.

---

[24]*The earliest indisputable example of religious art is the "Lion-man of the Hohlenstein-Stadel." It was an ivory figure of a human body with the head of a lion found in the Stadel Cave in Germany (c. 32,000 years ago). Cave paintings of the spiritual nature (e.g. horses with wings or other anthropomorphic drawings) have also been discovered that date back at least 35,000 years.*

ANDERSON SILVER

On the opposite side of the spectrum, the most devout theist will view this "spirit" within us as a gift given by an omnipotent and all powerful being that is beyond the laws of nature. Differing religions will disagree as to why and to what end this spirit exists, as well as what happens to it after death. But today, almost a whopping 60% of the world's population identifies themselves as a practitioner of a mono-theistic religion that would essentially believe our higher faculties (spirits) are a celestial gift.

Somewhere in the middle of the spectrum there are those who are spiritual, but do not adhere to the strict idea of a single all powerful and supreme being that guides it all. They may believe in many gods (polytheism, such as Hinduism or the ancient Greeks), a series of spirits or deities (for example paganism – which is also a form of polytheism), or other forms of all permeating connection/spirituality of the Cosmos (for example Buddhism or Pantheism).

Throughout the history of Homo Sapiens, most of the 100 billion people that have existed have subscribed to one of these broad categories of belief systems (ontologies) discussed above. So, which of these belief systems actually got it right? Atheism, Monotheism, polytheism or pantheism? If you are being rational and honest with yourself, you already know the answer.

We all have different backgrounds, knowledge, teachings, etc. so different ideas will resonate with different people. This means different words and different interpretations of the same words will make different sense to different people. Therefore, it would be naive (to say the very least) to think we can all agree on a singular definition of what the "something more" is or why we have it or where it is going. However, there are things we can all agree on unconditionally: We all have organic and biological bodies; and we all have this "something more" (our consciousness) within the confines of our fleshy bodies. We can also agree that the body needs upkeep and maintenance (food, water, sleep, healing, etc) and so does this consciousness (mental health, a purpose, existential answers, etc.).

So, let us further agree for the sake of discussion to refer to this extra bit within us as "the spirit" or "the soul." The care and maintenance of the extra bit, then, can be referred to as "spirituality." Now don't jump to conclusions and think about halos and wings and harps. We could have just as easily named the extra bit "tomato" and the practice of tending to it "tomatoism." We're just putting a label on concepts we already agree on. In the context of our discussion the words "spirit" and "spirituality" are labels. The important take-away here is that "the spirit" needs tending to just as much as (if not more than) our fleshy bodies.

> "Virtue is the health and beauty and well-being of the soul, and vice the disease and weakness and deformity of the same."
>
> -   Socrates

Further to the above, we can also agree that the spirit is not born to harm (no one is born evil) and that it feels good to cooperate. We are social animals after all. So, doing good is what the "soul" or "spirit" naturally wants to do. Whether a singular personalized god, a universal reason that permeates all, a cosmic spiritual balance of oneness, or complete randomness, it does not matter what you believe in as long as you strive to work towards the betterment of humanity (which includes bettering yourself as well). One would be hard pressed to argue against such logic. This would also explain why the majority of religions and philosophies have similar underlying precepts, regardless of time period or geographical location. These precepts have always been the care of the community through the practice of love, respect, tolerance, selflessness and benevolence.

Currently, you are still very much used to living with your animal mind in control. No matter where you are in your progression of spirituality or the pursuit of a tranquil life, you are falling into old habits and letting your primitive mind's "autopilot" take control. Over time, as you begin to think and respond more and more with your faculty of reason, you will recognize the capacity and tendency to be more forgiving of others. As a starting point, however, forgive yourself for being overly judgy of others.

Judging others is another one of those built in survival mechanisms that you have. The primitive hunter gatherer mind views the world as a zero-sum game. In that view of the world, someone else's gain in something means something less out there for us to gain, and so the body's mind gets jealous. Similarly, the animal mind instinctively thinks that someone else's shortcomings means better chances for us to gain or obtain, and thus survive. This is why humans love gossip and (unfortunately) find joy in the misery of others. These primitive instincts of the vessel are archaic and in today's world downright harmful!

> "How much trouble he avoids who does not look to see what his neighbor says or does or thinks, but only to what he does himself, that it may be just and pure. Look not round at the depraved morals of others, but run straight along the line without deviating from it."
>
> - Marcus Aurelius

But our nature is not just that of an animal. We are a social animal with a capacity for reason. Therefore, your nature would dictate your reason to want to help and cheer for the success of others as well. Since we are social (pack) animals, others' success improves the tribe's chances of survival, and thus your own survival. But don't forget, that the evolution of reason outpaced that of the physical one. So, your pure animal instincts (your monkey body) wrongly wants for others to fail, while your higher faculty (your capacity for reason) wants them to succeed. This is yet another clear example of your duality within at work.

> "It is in keeping with Nature to show our friends affection and to celebrate their advancement, as if it were our very own. For if we don't do this, virtue, which is strengthened only by exercising our perceptions, will no longer endure in us."
>
> - Arthur Schopenhauer

You exist in the body of a predominantly hairless ape, yet you are so much more than a mindless animal. You are a rational intelligent consciousness. Unfortunately, you are not a purely logical and emotionless being either. The fact is you have this duality within. The animal mind is in charge more often than not due to simple logistics of energy conservation within your body.

The real you (your rational ordinary mind) lives *in* the vessel's brain, and so it is susceptible to the body's instinctive, natural, chemical, hormonal and emotional responses. There is no changing this reality, so no shutting off the animal mind or removing yourself from the body or distancing yourself from its needs. All you can do is give it your best effort to keep your rational ordinary mind in the conversation that is your inner discourse (as in the conversation or debate between the two minds). But the body has an upper hand here. You instinctively take care of the body first. You eat food because the body is hungry, you sleep because the body needs rest, and you may even go beyond the bare minimum and work proactively to make your body better and healthier (for example, going to the gym).

But you often skip on making your rational mind fit and stronger. Your spirit, whatever it may be or wherever it is going, needs to be taken care of just as much as the animal body. You must identify your basic spiritual needs (like the basic physical needs for your body) and work on them, even more so than your body. Why more so? Because you prefer your rational ordinary mind to be in charge more often than the animal brute that responds with emotions. So, you must fuel and train your higher faculties to be more present. You are more than a monkey. You have this wonderful capacity for reason, so feed it, train it, fuel it, strengthen it, be thankful for it, and (as much as you can) use it.

"We offer the gods sacrifice because they gave us wheat and wine. But they have produced such wonderful fruit in a human mind, as part of their plan to bestow on humanity the true secret of happiness. Are we going to forget to express our gratitude to them on that account?"

- Epictetus

12 FIND YOUR MIND'S EYE AND CULTIVATE IT

Life is hard. You have things to do, responsibilities to take care of, bills to pay, jobs to get to, relationships to maintain...and somewhere in there you have to try and have some fun right? After all, if you're not enjoying life, what's the point? But have you ever considered that perhaps you have been seeking joy in the wrong places?

> "On every occasion I must ask myself this question, 'What have I now in this part of me they call the ruling principle?' "
>
> - Marcus Aurelius

The animal mind seeks sensory pleasures because these "cravings" are inherently coded in your DNA to give the animal body what it needs to survive (food, water, propagation of the species, etc). However, the primitive instincts of the animal body are no longer entirely necessary for your survival and, if anything, they are hurtful to your life in today's modern world. The part of your brain that understands this is your rational intelligent ordinary mind. This is the part of you that will watch things happen "from behind a viewing pane" and wonder in confusion how you can act in such a way, even though you know it's wrong. All animal vessels and their minds are the same and very much predictable in their behaviour patterns. Your capacity for rational thought, however, is the unique you. It is the part of you that thinks, sees, understands and contemplates.

> "[With respect to the voices within] we may fairly assume that they are two, and that they differ from one another; the one with which a man reasons, we may call the rational principle of the soul, the other, with which he loves and hungers and thirsts and feels the fluttering of any other desire, may be termed the irrational or appetitive, the ally of sundry pleasures and satisfactions?"
>
> -   Socrates

The body's mind is necessary and our partner in this journey we call life. However, it is an "autopilot" that has no capacity for contemplation or reason. It is a series of coded IF, THEN, THEREFORE[25] responses (instincts) that follow patterns. And

---

[25] *This series of predetermined coding that is in our DNA was discussed in detail in chapter 9 of* Your User's Manual *titled "Bad Coding." Emotions are essentially knee-jerk reactions based on pre-built "If," "Then", "Therefore" statements that are part of your core operating system.*

since the body's mind is an "autopilot," it does not have an end game. There is no end to its craving. There is no end to its wants. It will keep wanting until death. This is simply the way it is programmed, and we can't really change that.

> "Filling to fullness is not as good as stopping at the right moment. Over sharpening a blade causes its edge to be lost."
>
> -   Lao Tzu

The past cannot be modified. The future is undetermined. The only time you are actually living is when you, the real you, is interacting with the "Here and Now." There is nothing more, there is nothing less. The "Here and Now" is all you have ever had, and all that you will ever have. Your entire life can be summarized in a series of consecutive "Here and Nows."

Interacting with the "Here and Now" while using your rational mind offers you options and thought out responses. Conversely, interacting with the "Here and Now" using the "autopilot" is merely the act of going through the motions without being fully aware of or engaged with the world around you (think of the example of driving to a destination without ever being fully aware of what you were doing). The two variables that are truly necessary to live life to the fullest, then, is your faculty of reason (consciousness) and the "Here and Now."

"For the present is the only thing of which a man can be deprived, if it is true that this is the only thing which he has, and that a man cannot lose a thing if he has it not."

- Marcus Aurelius

In our reality, time has no pause button; neither does it have a rewind button. The "Here and Now" is a function of time, and you have no control over time itself. Therefore, of the two variables necessary to truly be alive, the "Here and Now" is the variable that sits firmly outside your domain of control. Engaging your rational ordinary mind to interact with the "Here and Now," however, is entirely within your control. Therefore, the key to a fulfilling life is not in how much you eat, travel, party, what you wear, where you go or what the world has to offer you. If you are like most of us, you know by now that chasing the sensory pleasure of the body (money, titles, possessions, relationships, etc.) has no end or lasting joy. You always want more, and this pursuit often brings problems with it. The key to a happy life, then, is simply in your capacity to engage your rational mind (the real you) in your "Here and Now."

"There is a Buddhist saying that trying to seek happiness through sensory gratification is like trying to quench your thirst by drinking saltwater...Sex is one such experience. But we can also experience happiness at the deeper level through our mind, such as through love, compassion and generosity...While the joy of the senses is brief, the joy at this deeper level is much longer lasting."

- Dalai Lama

This is all easier said than done. How do you engage your real self to be in the "Here and Now"? What can you do to better your chances of *living* as opposed to just *being* alive? The ancients tell us there is only one solution, which is straightforward: Train the part of you that you wish were more present...to be more present. Self-awareness is nothing more than understanding and being aware of your duality within and knowing which part of you needs to be cultivated, engaged and present. And so, mindfulness is simply the ability of keeping the faculty of reason focused on the "Here and Now."

"You've endured countless troubles - all from not letting your ruling reason do the work it was made for - enough already!"

- Marcus Aurelius

Try this for an exercise: Take a moment from reading this and look around. Identify five things that are visible that you were previously unaware of. It can be anything from a miniscule detail like a speck of dust on your sleeve to a giant cloud in the sky. After identifying five things, recognize just how much there is around you right now that you had not seen or noticed until you specifically looked for it. This new awareness comes from shifting the tunnel vision of the "autopilot" to the broad view of the rational intelligent mind. There are different forms of meditation, including the Stoic reflection of thought (e.g. writing in a journal) or the Buddhist Zen meditation, but they all have the same goal in common: Remove as much of the animal mind and it's distractions from your thoughts as possible, and focus on the real you and your mind's eye.

A useful meditation aid you can employ to help achieve this is the use of imagery. In my previous work, the imagery of the bridge and its pillars in the river was used to depict yourself (the real self) and the flowing river represented the flow of time. Time itself (the flowing waters of the river) contains everything external to your rational ordinary mind, including emotions, events, things, people, etc. Find some quiet time to speak to yourself and meditate on your mind's eye. Close your worldly eyes and focus on the river that is time. See everything that happens floating in the river that is time…all the good, bad, known, unknown is part of this flowing water that is time. It comes, it brushes up against you (the bridge's pillars in the water) and it flows by…past you and gone forever. But you remain. You are always there. All else changes, but you, the real you, the rational ordinary mind remains there…solid…watching all this go by you like the unmoving pillars of the bridge.

> "Time is like a river made up of the events that happen, and a violent stream; for as soon as a thing has been seen, it is carried away, and another comes in its place, and this will be carried away, too."
>
> -   Marcus Aurelius

As you repeat this meditation, you can echo a mantra that resonates with you as well. A common Buddhist mantra (for example) is to think "Bud" when you inhale and "Dha" when you exhale. The goal, once again, is to quiet down the animal mind and clear all its noise (wants, hopes, wishes and desires) from your thoughts. You are looking to focus on your true mind only. Through repetition of such exercises (much like resistance training of muscles in the gym), your higher faculty becomes more aware of itself and "plugged-in" to the present. Your ruling faculty becomes less dependent on the "autopilot" and more in touch with the real you, thus consciously interacting with the present. Simply put, you will cultivate the habit of using your rational ordinary mind. The key to achieving this is repetition. Whether it is from mindful meditation, reading, writing, etc., by repeating these axioms, your mind's eye (the real you) will become stronger, more active and present more often.

"We are what we repeatedly do, therefore, excellence is not an act but a habit"

- Aristotle

Be honest with yourself, have realistic objectives and don't lose motivation for lack of quick results. Remember that this exercise is not like a switch, as in you cannot apply this once and expect a change forever. Progress in the pursuit of a tranquil life is slow and a lifelong journey. Much like with anything else that is worth doing in life, it takes time and effort. Progress is slow, not easy, and it is not linear. There will always be steps back, and the "autopilot" will always be a part of your ruling faculty and your day to day. Moreover, you inevitably will be exposed to decrepit influences from your environment again and again. This is a certainty and outside of your domain of control. What *is* in your control, however, is how you treat, respond to and handle the distractions and occasional steps back, and your continued efforts to keep trying to improve.

> "...so keep yourself simple, good, pure, saintly, strong for your proper work. Fight to remain the person that philosophy wished to make you. Revere the gods and look after each other. Life is short - the fruit of this life is a good character and acts for the common good."
>
> - Marcus Aurelius

Think the way you want to be. Your body's "autopilot" (over time) will emulate your thoughts. It has long been known that forcing a smile for just 20-30 seconds can boost the production of chemicals and hormones associated with happiness (dopamine, serotonin, endorphins, etc.), thus actually modifying your feelings. Through repetition and discipline, you can change the way your animal mind operates to a certain extent. In this way, you can train your "autopilot" to be closer to virtue when you (the real you) shuts off and gives up the ruling faculty within. But to be able to practice this continued discipline and training, you have to be clearly aware of *who* is thinking and *what* it is thinking. So, spend time reflecting inwardly to wake up your mind's eye, your rational mind, your higher faculties. Don't let the distractions of the human affairs take you away from your true self.

"Such as are your habitual thoughts, such also will be the character of your mind; for the soul is dyed by the thoughts."

- Marcus Aurelius

Helen Keller was struck with an illness that left her deaf and blind before she was two years old. She lived (in her own words), as if she was "at sea in a dense fog." Most of us with sight and hearing would automatically assume that she was very unfortunate and a prisoner of her own mind. Just imagine the darkness, silence and confusion of trying to experience and learn the world around you without the capacity to see it, or ability to talk or communicate with others to hear about it…at 2 years old!

Hellen Keller, of course, would disagree. She even goes as far as to claim that she may have been more free than those of us who have sight and hearing, as we are constant slaves to our externals. She was more intimate with her mind's eye than most, as she spent less time distracted with external stimuli and more time "checking-in" with her rational mind. She depicts her sincere connection with herself (her real self) in a passage from her autobiography "The Story of My Life." She was the first blind and deaf person to earn a Bachelor of Arts Degree, which is a significant accomplishment. However, she shares some of her concerns (while at college) of not having enough time to be in touch with herself.

"Gradually I began to find that there were disadvantages in going to college. The one I felt and still feel most is lack of time. I used to have time to think, to reflect, my mind and I. We would sit together of an evening and listen to the inner melodies of the spirit, which one hears only in leisure moments when the words of some loved poet touch a deep, sweet chord in the soul that until then had been silent. But in college there is no time to commune with one's thoughts."

- Helen Keller

The lesson is clear. We do not spend enough time talking to ourselves, because we are so distracted by all that happens around us...external to us. Spiritual well-being is no different than physical well-being. It takes time, investment and discipline. Arnold Schwarzenegger was a superb physical specimen in his time. He won several bodybuilding competitions and found his way on to the silver screen from the dedication he gave his body. He was not granted this physical accomplishment by the wish of a genie or the snap of a finger. He used to spend five hours a day, every day, in the gym to gain the desired results. For anyone aspiring to have a physique like the Terminator, the requirements are simple: spend time in the gym. The more time you spend daily, the closer you will be to looking like Conan the Barbarian. For your average person, of course, a minor fraction of this regiment is more than enough to have a healthy physique. But the point is that whatever the final goal or objective, it can only be achieved through action, work and discipline.

"The person who wants to be good must not only learn the lessons that pertains to virtue, but train themselves to follow them eagerly and rigorously. Could someone acquire instant self-control by merely knowing that they must not be conquered by pleasures, but without training to refuse them?"

- Musonius Rufus

On the mental side, the required effort is no different. Lhamo Thondup is one of today's most prominent spiritual leaders. Also known as the 14th Dalai Lama, he has an outstanding mastery of his mind's eye and is more mentally present and mindful than most people in the world. His Holiness the 14th Dalai Lama did not attain this accomplishment by wishing upon a shooting star. He accomplished it through hard work and discipline. Even today at 84 years old, his holiness spends six hours a day, every day, meditating, praying, reading, writing and studying to reflect on his spirituality and his mind's eye. For the rest of us, the secret to freedom from mental perturbation is the same: Work on it. Invest the time to cultivate your mental fortitude. Sure, most of us don't have six hours a day to work on our spirituality like the Dalai Lama. However, would you agree that you could have easily carved out just 15 more minutes today to dedicate towards your mental well-being? Or thirty minutes? Or more?

"Aren't you ashamed to reserve for yourself only the remnants of your life and to dedicate to wisdom only that time can't be directed to business?"

- Lucius Annaeus Seneca

13 MANAGING YOUR INNER RELATIONSHIP

So, there it is dear reader; you have two personalities within you. This is a direct result of the separate evolutionary paths that your animal body and your higher faculties of reason and intelligence took. Recognizing this duality within is another positive step down the path of your pursuit of a tranquil life. Your next big step will be in learning to manage the relationship between the two distinct voices within you.

> "When, in the process of self-transformation, desires are aroused, calm them with nameless simplicity. When desires are dissolved in the primal presence, peace and harmony naturally occur, and the world orders itself."
>
> - Lao Tzu

Undoubtedly you would prefer to have your rational mind be in charge, present and engaged *all the time*. Never forget that this is impossible. We need the animal brain to survive. The "autopilot" has its time and place to save us from the burden of having to contemplate moral decisions over everything we do all the time (you do not need to consider the moral implications of taking another step while you walk right?). A fundamental error would be to try to suppress the animal, its emotions and reactions. Suppression is an exercise in futility. It is impossible. You cannot avoid emotions; neither can you exist without them, as your animal body comes with its own mind (it's a package deal), and you (the real you) cannot exist without the vessel you are in. So you're stuck with your proverbial roommate.

However, feelings *can be managed*. As an example, bravery is not the *lack* of fear, but rather it is the capacity to do what is necessary and right in the *presence* of fear. In the same way, the tranquility you seek is not the lack of emotions, but rather the capacity to remain in equanimity and have your rational ordinary mind engaged even in the presence of perturbed feelings and strong emotions.

> "But when a man's pulse is healthy and temperate,...he has awakened his rational powers, and fed them on noble thoughts and inquiries, ...after having first indulged his appetites neither too much nor too little."
>
> -   Socrates

Never forget you have a terminal disease. You were born with a death sentence like the rest of us. Your impending death is not a question of "If" but "When." Don't ignore this fact. Instead let this truth have a profound impact on your attitude towards life.

Don't let another day tick away in ignorance of the reality that you are a dying person living on limited and borrowed time…borrowed time that you can never get back once it is spent. Can today be the day you stop pretending otherwise? If so, you should give your greatest effort possible to live a good life and be alive. And keep in mind that "your best" is unique to you. There is no single standard "best" that all can strive towards. Each one of us has a different "best" given our objective realities. Just do *YOUR* best.

> "Let each thing you would do, say or intend be like that of
>   a dying person."
>   -   Marcus Aurelius

As part of your best effort, remember that you are only truly alive when your rational mind is engaged with the "Here and Now." Yes, it's true that you cannot turn off your "autopilot," but (and this is a big but) this does not mean you should blindly succumb to its whims, wants and wishes and watch your life pass you by in the pursuit of sensory pleasures. Where has that gotten you so far?

> "Every man lives only in the present…all the rest of his life
>   is either past or is uncertain. Brief is man's life and small
>   the nook of the earth where he lives."
>   -   Marcus Aurelius

If knowledge is freedom, you are now one step closer to it, as you are now firmly aware of the two distinct voices within you. You can begin (one small step at a time) to learn to consciously manage the two voices within, instead of being a hopeless passenger not knowing what you feel or why you acted a certain way. You no longer have to watch a disaster happen as a third party from behind a viewing pane. With the new knowledge you have gathered here, you now have the necessary tools to shed the shackles that hold your rational mind back. You, the real you, can now take more and more control of your very precious and limited time. You can cultivate your rational mind to be present and to interact with your "Here and Now" more and more often. You only have a couple of decades (at best) to do any real good in this world. Why would you waste it being an animal? What are you waiting for? Tick Tock. *WHAT* you do doesn't matter nearly as much as *HOW* you do it. You are a human-*BEING*, not a human-*DOING*. So, stop worrying about getting things completed, accomplished, earned, attained, obtained, said, given, taken, etc. Instead focus on yourself, inwardly and live life while making a series of good moral decisions using your rational ordinary mind in your "Here and Now" as much as possible. Stop trying to impose your will on the world and instead see yourself as fortunate to be on the receiving end of what the world has to offer.

"Fancy things get in the way of one's growth. Racing here and there, hunting for this and that - Good ways to madden your mind, that's all. Relinquish what is external. Cultivate what is within. Live for your center, not your senses."

- Lao Tzu

You do not *HAVE* to do anything. You *GET* to. Take a page out of Helen Keller's life and slow down, stop your animal body, close your eyes, and look inwards. Get in touch with your mind's eye and talk to it, write down your thoughts and check-in with your rational intelligent mind in your journal. Take care of yourself (your true self). Your mental well-being is the most important thing in the whole world. If you do not have a rational mind, nothing good will follow. Without a rational mind, you will be of no use to anyone, especially yourself.

> "The instincts are based upon the external things and sense. Don't live for your senses. But, when no idea arises, the right idea comes. That is the true idea, from your true self."
>
> - Lao Tzu

Your brain contains a built-in mechanism that is (by nature) designed to give higher priority to bad news. This is what the media feeds on and takes advantage of. This instinct was a competitive advantage in the Savannah. Shaving off a few seconds in detecting a predator to begin running away (first) gave the ancestors' animal vessels a better chance to get away and remain alive to pass on its genes. There are still other primitive and negative instincts that are built-in to your vessel since they offered a competitive advantage for our ancient ancestors (e.g. Pessimism, anxiety, fear, anger etc..), but these are no longer necessary in today's modern world, so don't let them take control of your ruling faculty.

"And let this truth be present to you in the excitement of anger, that to be moved by passion is not manly, but that mildness and gentleness, as they are more agreeable to human nature, so also are they more manly; and he who possesses these qualities possesses strength, nerves, and courage, and not the man who is subject to fits of passion and discontent. For in the degree to which a man's mind is nearer to freedom from all passion, in the same degree also is it nearer to strength: and as the sense of pain is a characteristic of weakness, so also is anger. For he who yields to pain and he who yields to anger are both wounded and both submit."

- Marcus Aurelius

In the same way that the animal vessel has its instincts, so does your consciousness. Your faculty of reason knows what the right thing to do is in almost all circumstances. Unfortunately, the rational mind and its intelligent ideas sometimes gets shut out by the louder voice within that comes from the animal mind (*"You totally deserve it...sit down, eat the pizza and watch TV!"*). But with the awareness of this discourse comes the capacity to ensure your rational mind can be just as loud. And don't stop there. Make your rational mind louder and more convincing than the arguments of your animal mind and its sensory pursuits. Take control of your inner dialogue...because you can.

"It is during our darkest moments that we must focus to see the light."

- Aristotle

Things happen one step at a time...one day at a time. Recall that you are only *truly living* if your real self is engaged in the "Here and Now." So as often as you can, be who you want to be. And as often as you can, act the way you know it to be right. Don't worry about your past decisions. Good or bad they are all history. Instead, remain focused on trying your best in your current "Here and Now." Focus whatever energy you have (no matter how little) in this moment and then the next...and then the next...on being the best person you can. That is all there is to being a good person living a good life. Do the right thing, right now, as often as you can. The pursuit of a tranquil and good life is not perfection. It is merely in reducing the number of times in which you are not present in the moment or not being who you want to be (i.e. mindfulness).

"The time is always right to do what is right."

- Dr. Martin Luther King Jr

You can never be perfect. There are no easy solutions to living a good life. There are only good solutions, and no matter how little or slow the progress may be, progress is progress, so give yourself a break. You must never be discouraged during times when you are not engaged with the "Here and Now." The animal "autopilot" will have more time being active than your rational intelligent mind will, despite what you would like to believe. This is simply a result of the biological function of the vessel in which you reside, not a reflection on the shortcomings of your efforts (again, give yourself a break). It is a simple game of energy conservation. So, don't judge yourself for not being your best or mindful 100% of the time. Just do your best as often as you can in your current "Here and Now." That is more than enough.

> "Let us therefore set out whole-heartedly, leaving aside our many distractions and exert ourselves in this single purpose, before we realize too late the swift and unstoppable flight of time and are left behind. As each day arises, welcome it as the very best day of all, and make it your own possession. We must seize what flees."
>
> - Lucius Annaeus Seneca

What will you manage to make of your day today before it slips through your hands and becomes part of the past forever? What will you do in this moment? You are all too often focused on the "To-Dos" and accomplishments and tasks you have. Why? Your rational mind understands that *HOW* you approach the task at hand is far more important than *WHAT* task you are approaching.

> "Our whole society has a materialistic culture. In the materialistic way of life, there's no concept of friendship, no concept of love, just work, twenty-four hours a day, like a machine."
>
> - Dalai Lama

Go back to your spiritual necessities[26]. These are your self-identified must haves to give you a purpose in life. Focus on your necessities instead of what our misguided Western society has told you to do (e.g. pursuit of money and possessions). What do you think will make your life better? Taking an hour in the morning to Meditate and jog for a healthy body and mind or go into the office an hour earlier to impress the "boss" and maybe get recognition for it and make more money.

> "If we look at today's materialistic life people seem mainly concerned with sensory experiences. So that's why their satisfaction is very limited and brief, since their experience of happiness is so dependent on external stimuli. When something good is happening, they are happy. Good food, they are happy. Good music, they are happy. When these things stop, then they feel bored, restless, and unhappy. Of course, this is nothing new. Even in the time of the Buddha, people would fall into the trap of thinking that sensory experiences would bring happiness. So, when joy arises at the level of your mind and not just your sense, you can maintain a deep sense of satisfaction for a much longer period of time."
>
> - Dalai Lama

---

[26] *Your necessities should be consciously and conscientiously identified by YOU and not "taught" by anyone else (including parents, society, spiritual leader, etc.) Once you identify your own spiritual necessities, life becomes easier to manage. Once you have a "Why?" the "How" becomes very easy. (Refer to chapter 14: from* Your User's Manual *for additional details.)*

14 A FEW MORE TOOLS

There are many tangible tools you can employ to help cultivate your faculty of reason. As you walk down this path that is your journey for the search of a tranquil life, you will find habits, exercise and meditations that work for *you*. Some ideas for such exercises were already shared in the preceding chapters (imagery of the bridge, Premeditatio Malorum, etc). However, before I end the book I will share a few more tools and techniques that have helped me in my own personal journey. Hopefully some, or all, might resonate with you and help you in your own spiritual progress. The goal of these exercises (and any other habits you adopt along the way) is ultimately to strengthen your faculty of reason and to train it so that your rational mind becomes engaged with your continuous cycle of "Here and Nows," more often.

"There is nothing noble in being superior to your fellow men. True nobility lies in being superior to your former self."

-   Ernest Hemingway

The first and most crucial point I want to share is journaling. Keeping a journal is your most potent tool in managing the inner discourse. Your animal mind is loud and persistent. You have to find ways to ensure your rational voice remains in the conversation. This is difficult at the best of times (when you are calm and have an emotionless ordinary mind) and impossible at the worst of times (when you are overwhelmed by emotions). When you are angry, fearful or anxious, you may feel like there is nothing else inside you...only afflicted emotions. But your rational mind is *always* there. It merely gets smothered.

"For the just man does not permit the several elements within him to interfere with one another, or any of them to do the work of others...And ought not the rational principle, which is wise, and has the care of the whole soul, to rule, and the passionate or spirited principle to be the subject and ally?"

-   Socrates

Writing in your journal can help you keep your rational mind's voice alive and active. When you physically write down your thoughts, it is more likely that you are engaging and using your faculty of reason. When you try and "think" and "reflect" in your mind, your "autopilot" can, and will, often hijack the thought process without you being aware of it. So, pick up a pen and paper (at least once a day) and write down your logical thoughts. If you can, keep a pocket journal that you can pull out and write a few words in any time you feel like you can/should. You will feel its impact and benefits almost immediately, which should help motivate you to do it more often. Just start somewhere.

> "Whether you're keeping a journal or writing as a meditation, it's the same thing. What's important is you're having a relationship with your mind."
>
> - Natalie Goldberg

Try micro meditations. Although Zen meditation for longer periods of time is highly effective and should be part of your regular routine, 1-5 minute meditations can be surprisingly effective. While in an elevator, sitting at your desk, in the shower, before getting out of your car, etc…any tiny fraction of time where you can close your eyes, focus on your mind's eye and clarify your thoughts and goals will dramatically improve your capacity to engage your rational mind in the "Here and Now." All it takes is to remind yourself that the real you is in there, amongst the jumbled mess of your thoughts. Remind yourself that you want to be engaged in the "Here and Now."

Remind yourself that when you feel angry, "you" don't actually feel angry. It is the body's mind that feels angry. The real you has no capacity for emotions and is independent from the emotions. The body's mind is your roommate. It is not you. You can't make emotions disappear, so when you feel that anger, it will remain there in your thoughts. But nothing stops you from reminding yourself that this anger is part of the vessel in which you reside, and that nothing in nature says it has to dictate your life. It can only dictate your thoughts if you allow it to. When you feel anxiety, fear, envy or sadness…remind yourself "you" in fact do not feel those. The animal mind does. "You" can still control the vessel in a manner that is not emotional and do the right thing (such as to forgive unconditionally), even while the body's mind screams to do otherwise. Equanimity is not the lack of emotions, but the capacity of your rational ordinary mind engaged even in the presence of perturbed feelings and strong emotions.

> "Act by act thou must build up thy life, and be content, if each act as far as may be, fulfils its end. And there is never a man that can prevent it doing this."
>
> -   Marcus Aurelius

Being mindful of your objective reality can also help you be more grounded in the present and help your rational mind engage with your "Here and Now." You can develop and use any anchoring practice that works for you. Personally, I carry a 2000-year-old ancient Roman coin with me that I reach for when disturbed or confused. It reminds me of my mortality, which in turn puts the world, my life and the events contained within into perspective. The goal is to wakeup the ruling faculty and jolt your "autopilot" out of the driver seat. Then you can get your rational mind to view your surroundings, your environment and your life in the context of the grand scheme of things. You are alive, and not for long. Don't waste any of it "coasting" through time due to a lack of effort on your part.

> "One day you will wake up and there won't be any more time to do the things you've always wanted. Do it now."
>
> -   Paulo Coelho

Something else that has helped me is to take a moment and look around. Identify five things that you otherwise would not have noticed. This does not have to be anything special. In fact, the more mundane it is, the more primordial its effect, as it brings a profound realization of *how much* you are missing-out-on from coasting through life on "autopilot". Just pick-up on something you might not have seen, heard, or felt. Do you see a fly? Think about the millions of flies that flew past you in your lifetime already, that you never noticed because you weren't looking. Do you hear the wind? Think about where this air comes from, how many times it has travelled around the world, how long it has existed, predating our existence here on this planet. Do you feel a part of your body you hadn't noticed before? An ache, itch or just simple awareness of ...say your left leg's calf muscle. Feel other muscles and parts of your body and marvel at this biological structure that is magnificent and beautiful. Think about this vessel you occupy, how your thoughts are intertwined with it, and how you are now aware of your body's mind and its separate existence.

> "Mindfulness isn't difficult. We just need to remember to do it."
>
> -   Sharon Salzberg

As a final tool, you can remind yourself regularly (as an exercise) why you do what you do. In chapter 4 I discuss how every action, large or small, begins with a moral decision. In some cases, the choice (to do or not to) has been made long ago (e.g. moving your foot forward while walking). In other cases, it takes a more involved contemplation (e.g. should I move for a new job). Whatever action you eventually take, is based on a moral decision or contemplation you made at some point regarding the action in question.

Recall that you do not *have* to do anything. You *get* to. If ever it feels like you have no choice in the matter, or that you feel forced to do something, simply remind yourself that you have forgotten why you chose to do this thing in the first place. Remind yourself these reasons and think about them. Perhaps after contemplation, you will realize that you no longer want to do it, as the variables or the premise has changed. Other times, reminding yourself of why you do what you do will give you the much-needed motivation to follow through on it without further resentment. It'll give you the kick you need to engage your higher faculties with the "Here and Now" and do what you have to with a happier disposition and a sense of conviction in what you do as opposed to feeling the drudgery of *"I hate this but I guess I should do it."*

"Dig deep within yourself, for there is a fountain of goodness ever ready to flow if you will keep digging."

-   Marcus Aurelius

If self-improvement is really something you want to pursue, why do you block off 8-10 hours a day 5 days a week to go to work, yet only read a few minutes here or there when it is "convenient"? Or why do you barely spend any time to think about the big questions, or spend time looking, exploring and talking internally? *"I don't have time"* never actually means a lack of time. It is merely a lazy way of saying *"This just isn't worth my time compared to all the other more important things I chose to spend my time on."* We put in inordinate amounts of time pursuing money. We chase vacations, weekends, parties and gatherings. We are a slave to our sensory pleasure thinking they are the source of happiness (how has that worked out for you so far?) The average person still finds time for 28 hours of TV per week. Have you spent more time watching TV or playing games this week, than you have reading, talking to yourself, writing in a journal, reflecting on your choices or meditating on your mind's eye? The things that will help you become better internally and mentally do not require anything external. Only your effort.

If self-improvement is truly what you seek...by now you already know what to do and how to begin the journey. You do not need to sit around and wait for a magic cure or a quick fix. listening to the right voice within: You...the real you...the rational intelligent mind. Listen to the right voice, no matter how much emotion the animal mind throws at your inner discourse. It is not a monologue, so don't let the body's mind speak alone. Work as best and as hard as you can to keep your rational mind in the conversation. How do you want to live the rest of your very short and finite life? Time is passing you by. *Tick Tock.*

ABOUT THE AUTHOR

After many years of misery, stress and search for meaning, ANDERSON SILVER through study, reflection and meditations found a tranquility he never thought possible. Periodically, Anderson shared some of his meditations with people around him having spiritual breakdowns, who also found inner peace through these thoughtful reflections. From this experience arose the series of books "Your User's Manual" and "Vol 2: Your Duality Within", which aims to help readers obtain the tranquility and purpose that we all seek. A graduate of Concordia University, Anderson is a CPA, a husband, and father of three. He resides in Montreal.

SUGGESTED READING

What is the point? What is the purpose of life? Why must I suffer the stress, and anxiety that comes with it? Why does it all seem so hard and so unfair? If you have asked yourself any of these questions, then you have found the book you are looking for.

There are answers to all of these questions and Anderson Silver has compiled teachings from Stoicism and other schools of thought in Your User's Manual. This refreshing collection not only gives the reader much sought after answers, but also provides tools for finding purpose, and living an anxiety-free life in the modern world. Meant as a light read that the reader can come back to and meditate on periodically, Anderson has done a wonderful job of condensing fundamental teachings, making Your User's Manual a straightforward read in answering life's most pressing questions and recognizing what is truly important.

Made in the USA
San Bernardino, CA
03 August 2020